Cruising Tips

from a

Professional Cruise Addict

A Complete Planning Guide with Cruise Planning Journal, Packing Checklist, Cruise Hacks, and Lots More for Your Perfect Cruise Vacation

Dr. Melissa Caudle

Cruising Tips & Hacks from a Professional Cruise Addict
Copyright © 2022 by Dr. Melissa Caudle

ALL RIGHTS RESERVED. Neither the publisher nor the author are responsible for the outcomes of the suggestions in this book, as it is being offered for educational purposes only. Before any travel, please check with a medical professional. Keep all travel documents safe and secure before, during and after any cruise. The transmission, duplication or reproduction of this work is in violation of the U.S. Copyright. Reprints are only allowed with the direct written consent from the publisher and/or author.

Publisher: Absolute Author Publishing House
Editor: Kathy Rabb Kittok
Cover Designer: Rebecca @rebecacovers
Author Headshot: Robby Cook Stroud
Photos: Taken by Dr. Melissa Caudle, Helen V. Ray, Robby Cook Stroud, Caylen Ray, Tina Rubin, Kelly Rae Caudle, and Roger Molina III, Blythe Cheatham during their many, many cruises.
Icons: Stock Photos used with permission from Microsoft Word

PAPERBACK ISBN: 978-1-64953-546-7
EBOOK ISBN: 978-1-64953-547-4

This book belongs to:

_____

The Happy Cruiser!

DEDICATION

To my mom and dad, who took me on my first cruise, and I never stopped, and to my forever cruising sisters, Caylen and Robby. Mom, we're keeping our promise and we are cruising. I don't think you meant once a month, though.

Dr. Mel's parents, Bill and Helen Ray, on the Carnival Conquest December 2003.

Dr. Mel's mom, Helen V. Ray, who exposed her to the love of cruising - August 2011.

Warning: Cruising can be habit forming. LOL. Stopping too early can be depressing!

Dr. Mel in September of 2021 on the Carnival Valor.

Table of Contents

INTRODUCTION	*1*
HOW TO BOOK A CRUISE AND FIND THE BEST DEALS	*5*
PAYING FOR A CRUISE	*17*
CRUISE DOCUMENTATION	*22*
CABIN CATEGORIES AND DECKS	*25*
WHAT NOT TO DO IN YOUR STATEROOM	*34*
THINGS YOU DON'T NEED TO BRING ON A CRUISE	*39*
CRUISE HACKS	*44*
MUST HAVES FOR CRUISING DURING COVID	*48*
DECORATING YOUR CABIN AND/OR YOUR DOOR	*63*
PACKING YOUR BAGS	*66*
TRAVELING WITH CHILDREN	*70*
ACTIVITIES ON BOARD FOR KIDS	*87*
BEST CRUISE LINES FOR KIDS	*89*

EXCURSIONS	97
BEVERAGES PACKAGES	100
SPECIALTY DINING	108
BONUS CRUISE PACKING HACKS	110
WHAT TO DO IF YOU GET SICK ON A CRUISE	112
BEFORE YOU GO, GIRL	114
CRUISE PLANNING GUIDE	117
PACKING CHECKLIST	119

INTRODUCTION

Hello! I'm Dr. Mel, and I love cruising. I am a self-proclaimed cruise addict with five decades vacationing on cruise ships and hopefully five decades more. There is something about boarding the enormous cruise ship, getting to my cabin, throwing my things onto the bed, and heading out to the Lido Deck for the sail away party. Of course, along the way, my sisters and I always stop at the buffet. It seems as if I left all my troubles behind as I sail away the moment I hear that booming ship's horn. For me, t doesn't matter the port or the number of days. Rather, I love being on the ship, not worrying about cooking, cleaning, working, figuring out where to eat, or what to do for entertainment. Everything is built right in for me to partake. I can take part in every activity or hibernate in my cabin. It's up to me. It's about the journey and making memories and not the destination.

With that said, booking a cruise is the simple part. Packing and planning for it are entirely different. I know because I have logged in my fair share of sea days and cruises. In fact, at the time of me writing this book, I have cruises booked each month for the next year with my sisters and since they lifted the Pandemic restrictions; we have already sailed fourteen months in a row. They are cruise addicts too and my sailing BFFs. My cruise companions have included my parents, grandmother, sisters, brother, my children, my grandchildren, nephews and their wives, great nephews and nieces, sister-in-law, future in-laws, and friends.

Dr. Mel's family on Royal Caribbean December 2003. Pictured are Caylen, Bill, Robby, Dr. Mel, and seated, Helen.

I have sailed on most cruise lines, including Royal Caribbean, Norwegian, Carnival, The Princess Cruise, MSC, Celebrity Cruises, Crystal Cruises, Holland America Line, Regent Seven Seas Cruises, and Windstar Cruises over a fifty-year period. I have seen a lot of changes over the years, some I miss and others I am elated they implemented. One I endeared and miss, is the formal Captain's party that once was held on formal night. The band played on stage and a dance floor was provided. Today, I can't listen to  the song by Luther Vandross, *Dance With my Father Again*, without crying fond tears. I will always cherish the times I danced with my father on these nights as now new memories I cherish form each time I cruise. My last cruise, I had the honor of dancing with my twelve-year-old grandson, Roger, during his first cruise. My memories continue and your memories to make are just around the next journey on your cruise.

I am a VIP loyalty program member on most cruise lines, having been on so many. One thing is for certain: I know the tips, tricks, and cruise hacks. If you're planning your first cruise or your thirtieth, this book is for you as I filled it with my tidbits of advice including how to get the best deals, what to pack, cruise hacks, and a list of cruise essential must-haves.

Bon voyage and happy sailing.

Hope to see you on the high seas, and, if you see me on a cruise, say "Hi!" I love to meet other cruise addicts and first-time cruisers.

Dr. Mel

Dr. Mel in January 2021 on the Carnival Vista.

How to Book a Cruise and Find the Best Deals

Dr. Mel enjoying the deck activities on the Carnival Ecstasy, February 2021.

Are you planning on a cruise soon? Is your mind boggled what cruise line or destination to choose? Do you want the best bargain for your cruise vacation? Who doesn't want the best deal possible when planning a vacation, especially a vacation on the high seas? Cruise ships are like mini cities and are self-contained. The price of the ticket covers everything for you except the adult alcohol beverages, but they have packages for that. Who doesn't want to be free of their everyday responsibilities and forget about cooking and cleaning?

It didn't take me long to figure out that I love cruises and they are my happy place. So, where are the best deals and how do you find them? How do you know which cruise line you want to venture off sailing to the Caribbean or Mexico? What about the islands? Europe, anyone? Just about anywhere in the world, you can find a cruise and a cruise bargain if you know where and how to look. Here are my tips for finding the best cruise deals.

1. **Search and research.** Search the internet for various vacation sites such as Vacations to Go, Cruise.com, Travelocity, Orbitz, and Priceline. Also, use Google to search using the keywords "Last minute cruise deals" as most cruise lines have them. Cruise ships want to fill up their open cabins, so they offer these deals, too. The only problem, sometimes you have twenty-four hours or fewer to book them or they are gone forever.

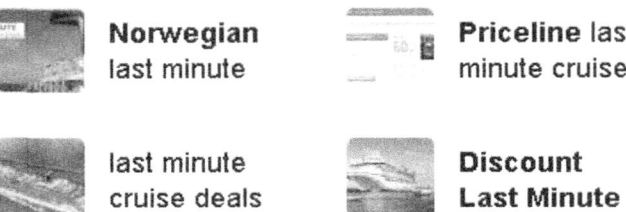

2. **Cruise line's website.** Go directly to the cruise line's booking webpage and join their membership program, often called VIP programs, Past Guest Loyalty Program, or Captain's Circle. Why? You will get deals dropped into your mailbox. My last cruise, six days to Belize, Costa Maya, and Cozumel, they assigned me an aft balcony. My price – FREE, with the only exception of paying taxes, port fees, and the staff gratuity in advance, which totaled $169. Yes, you read that right, an aft balcony cost me $28.16 a day. I can't stay home and eat for that. Also, as a VIP member, they mail me deals all the time. The cruise before that one, another aft balcony, was $229 for a seven-day cruise. Again, heck of a deal. Look at this recent deal I received from the Carnival Cruise Line.

3. **Use Twitter to get savings and discounts.** That's right, Twitter. Often travel agencies will tweet their last-minute offers. The ones I follow on Twitter are.

    ➢ Cruisedeals.com @cruisedeals,
    ➢ Cruise.com @cruisecom, and
    ➢ Best Travel Deals @cruisedealsbtd.

4. **Book early.** There is merit in booking early. During the high-season cruising, last-minute deals are hard to find. These include summer travel, school holiday period, and major holidays such as Thanksgiving, Christmas, and New Year's Eve cruises. So, if you're like me, and want to be on a specific floor or in a specific cabin, book early. You might not get the price discount, but you get the cabin you want. My last three cruises, I have stayed in the same aft balcony cabin and have had the same cabin steward. It really makes a difference for an addict cruiser like myself because it is like my home away from home and I know the cabin, the ship, and my steward. Here is the big tip.

About a week before I sail, I'll directly call the cruise line and inquire about any promotions they may have. When they see I am a VIP cruiser, they often give me perks, such as a free massage, dinner reservations at their private steak house, or a free excursion. I have even been bumped up to a larger suite, and I didn't even ask. Oh, then I ask if the price has dropped since I first booked the cruise. Most likely the answer will be, "Yes." That's when I ask if I can either have a credit to my cabin, or if they can refund the difference. Most cruise lines offer a built-in price guarantee that if you find a lower price, they will pay you the difference. This isn't automatic, and you have to do some investigating, but once the cat is out of the bag, they have no choice but to credit your account. So, be diligent and watch for the price drop and then go for it. You have nothing to lose and money to gain.

5. **Be flexible in your schedule.** If you can book at the last minute, you often get the better deals because cruise lines want to fill their cabins. This is especially important if you live in a cruise port town like me. I only live about twenty minutes from the cruise terminal, and I can get on a ship within one hour's notice. Yep! Believe it or not, I don't even unpack my cruise bags. Wait, don't say, "Yuck!" All of my clothes are clean. Because I am at a high level in my loyalty VIP program, I get three bags of laundry cleaned and folded on the ship for free. So, I always send my dirty clothes, wet bathing suits, etc., to be laundered the day before the cruise ends. Everything comes back to me folded and ironed. Packing is a breeze and since I cruise once a month, I just don't touch my bags, put them in the laundry room and wait until the next cruise. Now, before I leave again, I may change my formal dress or something so I can take pictures wearing a different outfit, but that is it. I stay ready to cruise.

6. **Join a land casino player's club.** I know this may sound strange as an option for cruise deals, but many land-based casinos are connected to cruise lines. If you play table games and slot machines frequently, you can contact the cruise line with your player card and often you will receive discounted

or free player rates for a cruise. An added bonus, if you decide to gamble on board, you will receive free cocktails while you are playing, and future cruise deals will pour in for you. So, be sure to check out this option.

Casino on the Glory. Join the Players Club and received perks.

7. **Laundry.** All cruise ships have a laundry room on each floor for your use. On Carnival, as I previously mentioned, if you are a Platinum or Diamond level cruiser, as a perk, they will do up to three bags of laundry for free. So, what do you do if you aren't a high-level VIP? Cruise ships have laundry facilities, so I did my laundry the day before I left. I never have enjoyed bringing home dirty laundry. I suggest you bring your own laundry detergent and fabric softener, so you don't have that expense of buying it on board. It can cost up to $7.00 a load if you don't bring your detergent.

Dr. Mel enjoying a day at the beach in the Bahamas, December 2021.

Dr. Mel with JC, the Assistant Cruise Director on the Ecstasy, May 2022.

8. **Cabin guarantee is important.** What does that mean? Basically, the cruise line guarantees you will get the cabin category you specified at the time you booked it. The only drawback is that you don't get to pick the deck you want or if you want in the bow, middle, or aft. So, if that is important, you will want to book the offer where you can pick your cabin

location. On that note, I have booked a single room interior cabin, frequently, when I wanted a private room and not share with one of my sisters, who are also VIP cruisers. Every time I have done this, they upgraded me to either an Oceanview room or a balcony for no additional cost. That may have more to do with the level of VIP member I am. But it is something to consider.

9. **Group travel.** To save money, travel with a large group. Most cruise lines offer free cabins to the group organizer if they book five cabins. Think about that for a large family reunion.

10. **Consider shoulder season sailings.** What on the high seas is that? Basically, it is the lower booking seasons, such as in April or late September for an Alaskan cruise, or March for the Mediterranean and October through February for the Caribbean.

11. **Isolate military, senior, and residency rate discounts.** Most cruise lines offer discounts to military personnel and seniors through AARP. Also available, but most people don't know is isolating the Residency Rate discounts. What this means is that a formula is used that requires port cities to book a certain amount of its residents for the revenue stream. They don't want us to know that. So, if you inquire with a cruise line if their Residency Rate quota has been met, they will more than likely give you a huge discount. That is how I got my last cruise for free. Remember, the answer is always, "No!" until you ask. There is no harm in asking, right.

12. **When all else fails, use a travel agent.** Why? Travel agents work with cruise lines and purchase in bulk directly from them. This allows them to give their customers discounts. If

you get in good with your travel agent, they will keep you in the loop of upcoming bargains. Here's something you need to know. If you book with a travel agent, if you incur difficulties before or during boarding, a cruise line representative will not be able to help you. They will defer you to your travel agent. Keep this in mind, as your travel agent earns a commission, rightfully so, to answer your questions and deal with any happenstance.

13. **Book your next cruise while you're onboard.** That's right. You can often get the best deals by booking your next cruise before you leave the one you're on. That's how I keep getting the same cabin and same cabin steward and great deals. The perks here often include great discounts, onboard credit up to $100 per cabin, free beverage packages, no-risk bookings, and often room upgrades. Check it out. Since COVID-19, Carnival no longer has this option, but they will email you fantastic deals before, during and after your cruise, so be on the lookout for those. It's a great way to cruise and save at the same time.

Tina and Dr. Mel at pool sail away party, May 2022 on the Ecstasy.

Cruising Tips & Hacks from a Professional Cruise Addict

Dr. Mel in August 2021 on cruise for the first time after lockdown.

Dr. Mel on Cruise 2005 immediately after Hurricane Katrina.

Paying for a Cruise

My cruise jar decorated with the help of my granddaughter.

I wish I could say that all cruises are free, but they're not. I don't know many people who have money to burn, so saving for a cruise or multiple cruises is key. When I first started cruising, I was a schoolteacher and wasn't making that much money; more like $8,000 per year back in the 1980s. So, I did everything I could to pinch pennies to go on a cruise. Instead of buying my lunch, I brought it from home. I never purchased expensive coffee but drank coffee from the teacher's lounge. If I found a penny, nickel, dime, or quarter, or had an extra dollar bill, I placed it in my jar earmarked "Cruise Money." In time, everything added up. Now, I have another jar my granddaughter helped me with my picture, so I can dream the dream, and we decorated it with stickers. She decorated her own jar too as she plans on cruising again with me in the near future and wants money for video games, etc. So, the tradition lives.

My granddaughter's cruise jar money. She is on a mission.

One of the best things I did in my career was to subscribe to a vacation fund through my school system. They also had a Christmas fund I could contribute. Both programs took out $25 a paycheck and put it into a savings account. Then, the Monday after Thanksgiving, they would send me a check. This money was what I spent on Christmas gifts and for my vacation the next year. It worked.

Then, I retired from the school system. However, I was in the habit of saving, so I started my Cruise Savings Account with my bank. Every week, I added money to it. Sometimes, $5, other times $25. No matter what, I had a cruise fund and I still do.

Cruising Tips & Hacks from a Professional Cruise Addict

When the 2019 COVID Pandemic hit, my cruising days were over because of the lockdown. That didn't keep me from keeping my Cruise Fund active. In fact, basically, it tripled. Why? First, I couldn't go on cruises during a two-year period. Talk about withdrawals for a cruise addict. So, instead, I kept adding to the account so that when the lockdown was lifted, I would have the money to cruise. After two years, I had enough money in that account to purchase eight cruises. This only encouraged me to keep adding to my account. Now you know how I am going on a cruise a month for the next year.

It takes discipline to save money for cruises and the other expenses. But, with time and diligence, you can. Remember, "If there's a will, there's a way."

With all of this said, you need to establish a budget so that other areas of your home finances aren't interrupted or become burdensome. I think it is important that we balance our finances and not overextend the budget for cruising. That is why I don't charge my cruises or finance them. I save and pay for them. When you charge a cruise or finance them, the cost is more because of the interest you are required to pay. So, don't! Save, save, and save. Then, find your "Dream Cruise Vacation." Then save, save, and save until you have the money for your cruise of a lifetime. Every penny counts and they add up fast.

Some cruise lines offer their membership credit cards that have significant benefits. In fact, I use my Carnival Master Card all year long to garner points I can use for cruises and shore excursions. The goal here is that everything I charge is paid off that month, actually that day, so I don't incur interest fees. This card also offered a $250 sign-up bonus after the first purchase, which was enough to pay for one of my cruises. Other credit cards offer points as well that can be transferred to cruise ship purchases.

Robby, Dr. Mel's sister, and her winning the VIP ENTERTAINER PACKAGE. If you have a chance to be one, participate in the game. Lots of bonuses for you.

I loved this balcony. This was on my 64th birthday cruise with my sisters.

Dr. Mel on Mardi Gras Cruise February 2022 with Sisters, Robby and Caylen. We always try to wear something thematic for specialty cruises. These are our Mardi Gras jogging suits.

Cruise Documentation

When you travel on a cruise ship, more than likely the itinerary will take you out of your country. This means that you will need the proper documentation for travel, which includes your passport and/or birth certificate and another form of state issued identification such as a driver's license. If you don't have a passport, apply for it early as it can take you several months to receive it. Also, your passport must not expire during the cruise you are on, or you will encounter difficulties disembarking during customs. Here is the list of documents you will be required to have to board a cruise ship.

- Passport
- Birth Certificate
- Driver's License
- COVID Negative Test
- COVID Vaccine Card
- Boarding Pass

Other documents you will want to keep safe and have readily available are:

- Cruise Boarding Pass
- Luggage Tags
- Health Insurance Card
- Flight Boarding Passes if applicable
- Hotel Information
- Travel Insurance
- Document holder/money belt

Hard Copy vs Verifly and Other Apps

Some cruise lines allow you to use apps on your phone such as Verifly or in my state, Louisiana, LAWALLET to upload your required travel documents. However, please be cautious and know that these aren't always foolproof. My case in point is my daughter and her fiancée were denied boarding on a recent cruise because they did not bring the hard copies of their driver's license, COVID vaccine card, and birth certificates. They thought because they used LAWALLET, the official app the state of Louisiana, they would be fine. However, they were rejected boarding because they did not have the hard copies of those legal documents with them. They were denied boarding because the cruise line won't accept LAWALLET or other state's apps that do the same thing. They then tried to use Verifly, but that had to be completed by midnight the night before sailing.

Cruise Hack Tip: Don't wait until the last minute to get your documents in order. Be ready and ALWAYS take your hard copy of your legal documents to avoid being denied boarding. I start a week in advance.

Cruise Hack Tip: For ease of boarding and debarkation, using your passport is the easiest and safest way to prove your citizenship. The lines at customs are quicker and less cumbersome. So, if you don't have a passport, I highly recommend that you apply for one and give yourself plenty of time to receive it.

Cruise Hack Tip: Cruise lines only accept valid passports, and your passport cannot expire while you are on a cruise. Therefore, if your passport will expire, renew it immediately, as it can take weeks for your new one to arrive in the mail.

Dr. Mel on a cruise in 1999.

Dr. Mel on the Carnival Ecstasy, March 2022; her 64th Birthday Cruise with sisters. That is the port of Progresso in the background, which is the longest cruise port in the world.

Cabin Categories and Decks

Dr. Mel in front of one of decorated doors. Cruise Ship Ecstasy on May 19, 2022.

Every cruise ship has cabin categories, and yes, some are better than others. Each one offers something different as well as different square footage, views, and balconies. So, what is the difference, and should you shell out extra money for a balcony or a suite? What about being able to choose the location of your room? Do these matter to you?

Cruise cabins or staterooms differ from hotel rooms. In fact, don't expect your cabin to be like a hotel room, and to be frank, hotel rooms are more user friendly, but with a few hacks and tricks of the trade you can make the most of your small stateroom. After many, many cruises, I eventually learned them, but I'm saving you lots of time not having to research message boards or through self-discovery.

Taken from my balcony room. I love getting a balcony on a cruise ship. If you have the funds, I highly recommend it.

Cabin Categories

Like hotels, cruise ships offer a variety of staterooms, also known as cabins, which accommodate your budget. How do you know which one is right for you? The answer here isn't easy and often is determined by your budget. Inside or interior rooms offer the cheapest rates, whereas the suites are the most expensive. Everything in between depends on your budget. Keep in mind that no matter which cabin category you book, your food, some beverages, activities, and the shows are always free. No worries there. Here is the lowdown on the categories of staterooms.

Inside/Interior Cabin

Inside cabins are usually smaller and are available from the first floor up to the top. The smaller ones will only allow for single occupancy whereas, some of the larger one allow for up to four people depending on the cabin's configuration. If a single, most likely you will have a twin bed, one closet, and a bathroom. Other interior rooms will have bunk beds or two single beds that can convert into a queen. When you book your cruise, you will be able to look at each configuration and chose the best option. An interior room will not have any view of the ocean, or a window, for that matter.

Porthole

A room with a porthole is much like the interior rooms, except there is a small round window that allows you to see outside.

Oceanview

Usually, the same configuration as an interior room but with a large viewing window so that you can see outside.

Balcony

Much like the staterooms of the interior or Oceanview, a balcony room offers the cruiser the ability to relax on a private balcony. There are different levels of balcony rooms, ranging from a partial obstructive view to an aft balcony, which is my favorite stateroom of all.

Suites

As with the balcony rooms, there are also different levels of suites available on a cruise ship which offers more room and luxury and spectacular views from a private balcony.

Front, Middle, Back of the Ship (Aft)

Location is key. How do you know if you want a room in the front, back or middle of the ship? I have had staterooms in all. The decision should be made according to what you like or want to do. The back of the ship is usually the quietest, whereas the middle is the noisiest because it is closer to all the activities.

The front of the ship is usually closer to all the entertainment and dining but are most affected by the waves and can get a little rocky during high seas. If you are worried about getting seasick, then usually staterooms in the back are the best.

Decks

Some cruise ships have fourteen or more decks. Wow! They are mini cities on the water. How do you know what deck you want your cabin? Again, that depends on pricing and location. If you want closest to the pool and outdoor parties, you will want decks seven and up. If you want closest to dining and entertainment, you will want floors three, four, and five.

Dr. Mel on the Carnival Ecstasy. Look at the lanyard around her neck. She collects the pins from each ship she has been on. The ones shown are those that fit. Of special note, the Rolls Royce pictured was removed off the Ecstasy June 18, 2022 and will be put on display on a new ship as the Ecstasy will no longer be in the Carnival fleet as of October 2022.

This is the promenade deck on the retired Ecstasy, which was my favorite Fantasy class ship that Carnival commissioned.

Cruising Tips & Hacks from a Professional Cruise Addict

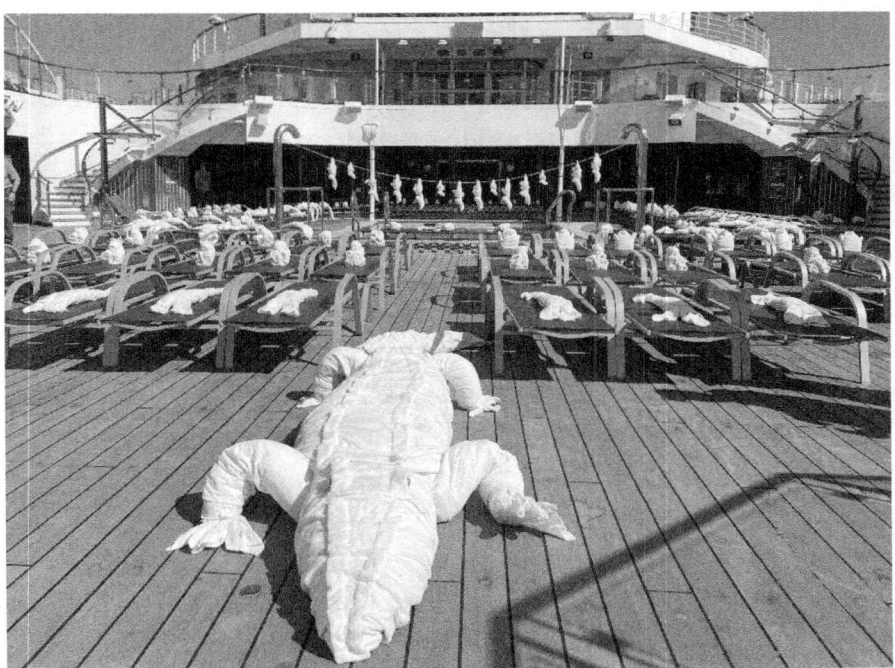

Animal creature left on our bed. Also, on some days, as a surprise, animal creatures are everywhere. You have to get up early to catch a site of those. They are so much fun!

What Not to Do in Your Stateroom

Your stateroom, once assigned, is your hideaway and private area on the cruise ship. However, it comes with a set of rules and regulations and there are certain things that are forbidden. As a cruiser, it is your responsibility to read all cruise line's rules and regulations before you sail. If not, you could face hefty fines and penalties or kicked off the ship. Here are the things you must never do in your stateroom.

1. **Smoke.** Smoking of any kind, including vape pens, is strictly forbidden in your stateroom or on your balcony. Face it. Cigarettes and pipes are a fire hazard. No, the cruise line isn't going to forbid you from getting your nicotine fix. They have designated areas on the ship, usually on the lobby floor, and tenth floor above the Lido Deck. So, if you are a smoker, check out their smoking areas and adhere to the rules to avoid penalties. If you are caught smoking, you will be fined up to $500 and possibly be kicked off the ship at the next port. So, it really isn't worth violating this rule.

2. **No open flames.** That's right. You can't burn candles in your room – period. Again, it is a fire hazard. To get around this, hack hint, you can opt to bring a battery-operated candle to create the ambiance you desire. Additionally, you cannot burn incense, have a hot plate, etc. Think in terms of high heat as a fire hazard. Now, cruise lines will allow you to bring a curling iron or flat iron, but DO NOT leave them plugged in when you leave your cabin. The steward will confiscate them.

3. **Hair dryer.** Do not bring a hair dryer and don't expect to dry your hair in the cabin's bathroom. First, the only outlet available is at the desk area outside of the bathroom and cruise lines supply the hair dryers. There is one outlet in the bathroom, but it is for shaving, and the plug will not fit a hair dryer. That's cruise life.

4. **Balcony door.** Don't leave the balcony door open. I know this is a tough one. Who doesn't want to listen to the ocean waves with the balcony door open? The main reason is that it will cause your cabin's air conditioning to work harder or freeze up and it also disrupts other cabin's air conditioning by yours. One unusual happenstance of propping your balcony door open is that it often sets off the fire alarm, causing panic. The last thing you need is for security to show up at your cabin door. Also, if the balcony door is open, and someone opens your cabin's entry door, the wind tunnel is massive, which makes a tremendous mess inside your room with papers flying everywhere.

5. **Hanging out wet things.** Never hang your wet bathing suits or beach towels on the balcony to dry. It may be tempting, but they fly away even if you use towel clips to secure them.

Rather, most cruise ships provide a drying line that expands in the shower for you to hand your wet items to dry.

Cruise Hack Tip: I bring magnetic hooks and scatter them throughout the cabin to hang my wet things on to dry.

Dr. Mel, on the right, and her daughter Kelly, enjoying the sun on a Mother's Day cruise, May 2022.

Dr. Mel with daughter Kelly in 2003 for her graduation present on the Carnival Conquest.

6. **Perfume.** Avoid spraying perfume or hairspray in your cabin. There is poor ventilation, and the results aren't pretty. Also, there are many people who suffer from chemical sensitivity and are bothered by perfume on a closed ship.

7. **No theft.** Don't steal the bathrobes or towels. These are amenities and if you take them, you will be charged for them.

8. **Decorating.** Don't tape anything to the walls or doors, as it can cause damage when removed.

   Cruise Hack Tip: Cabin walls are metal; thus, magnets stick to them.

9. **Valuables.** Don't leave your personal cash, ID's, passports, and medicine lying about. Instead, use the safe in the room and keep them protected.

Dr. Mel with her husband Mike on his first cruise in 1996.

Dr. Mel and Mike, her spouse, on a 2021 New Year's Eve Cruise on the Carnival Glory. One of only three cruises Mike has ever taken with her in their 39 years of marriage. Oh, we won the Love and Marriage Show.

Things You Don't Need to Bring on a Cruise

The worst thing you can do before your cruise is over pack. Trust me, I did it all the time until I got to my system of staying packed. Here is a list of items you do not need to pack to free up extra space.

1. **Toiletries and soap.** Cruise lines provide you with soap and shampoo. You will need to bring your conditioner. Unless you are allergic to specific products, you don't have to pack these, and these toiletries are replaced daily by your cabin steward.

2. **Hair dryer.** Cruise lines provide hair dryers which are located at the desk area in the drawer.

3. **Beach towel.** You really don't need to bring your favorite beach towel. All cruise lines supply beach towels in your room as well as at the swimming pools. You can even bring them off the ship when you dock at ports. Be sure to keep up with them because if you lose them or don't return them, you will be charged.

   Cruise Hack Tip: I purchased a very lightweight absorbent microfiber towel that rolls up and repels sand. I use this for my excursions because they are less bulky and weigh less, and dry quicker.

4. **A laundry bag.** Cruise lines supply laundry bags for each cabin. Typically, they are for sending your laundry out to be done, but there is nothing stopping you from using them for your dirty laundry.

5. **Something to read.** All cruise ships have a library with plenty of books for you to borrow. Again, saving your luggage space.

6. **Snacks, chips, candy, etc.** Trust me, you won't go hungry on a cruise ship and there are plenty of desserts and ice cream available. So, save the space for something more important.

7. **Don't bring hard liquor.** Cruise lines will confiscate your hard liquor, but they will allow two bottles of wine or champagne per person in each stateroom.

8. **Pillows and blankets.** You do not need to bring a pillow or blanket as there are plenty of them. If you need more, ask your steward and they will be provided. Cruise hack hint: Ask your steward for one of their soft fuzzy blankets to use on the balcony or upper decks during cold spells. I love the ones Carnival supplies and they come in all sizes. They are so cozy.

9. **Exercise equipment.** Don't bring your exercise equipment. You can leave your yoga mats and rubber bands at home as cruise lines have a complete workout facility.

10. **Weapons.** Don't' bring weapons, ammunition, firearms, or replicas of such of any kind. You will go to the brig.

11. **Illegal drugs.** Don't bring illegal drugs or medical marijuana. It may be legal in the state you are leaving from, but they won't be in the new country you are visiting.

12. **Sharp objects.** Don't bring sharp objects such as scissors or knives.

Dr. Mel with Tina, her best friend, on Ecstasy Cruise Ship, May 2022.

13. **Things that burn.** Don't bring candles or incense. You can't burn them on the ship. Don't bring flammable liquids or explosives.

14. **Sporting goods.** Don't bring baseball bats, hockey sticks, cricket bats, bows, and arrows, as they are considered weapons.

15. **Appliances.** Don't bring small appliances such as hot plates, coffee makers or curling irons. They are considered a fire hazard and will be confiscated.

16. **Riding toys.** Don't bring skateboards or surfboards. They are not allowed.

17. **Don't bring art supplies.** Paints can explode and catch on fire.

Dr. Mel with Tina enjoying an after-dinner cocktail on the Ecstasy, May 2022.

Dr. Mel in Belize 2018.

Dr. Mel on October Halloween Cruise 2021 with sisters Robby and Caylen.

Cruise Hacks

Face it, your cabin or stateroom is small, even if it is a suite. To make the most usage of your cabin and create extra storage, use these hacks.

1. **Metal hooks.** Use magnetic metal hooks throughout your stateroom to hang sweaters, bathing suits, umbrellas, hats, etc.

2. **Over the door shoe organizer.** This isn't just for shoes, but you can add space to your bathroom for all your toiletries, cosmetics, jewelry, hairbrushes, face masks, and other personal items. If traveling with an infant or toddler, these

are perfect to keep the baby's things organized from diapers to bibs to bottles to a quick change of clothing.

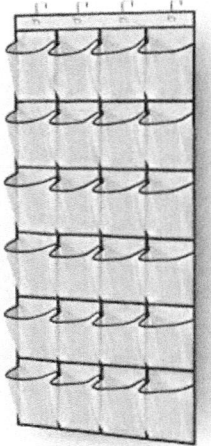

3. **Suction hooks for the shower.** If you want to hang more stuff to dry in the shower, bring suction hooks or a small shower basket with them to hang on the shower. This will keep things nice and organized.

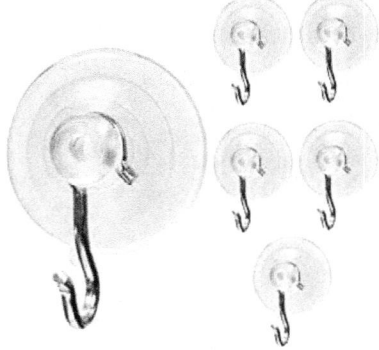

4. **A small car air-freshener.** Odors occur in bathrooms and if you want to always have a fresh-smelling one, bring along a hanging car air freshener. I prefer the lemon or citrus scent and place it in the bathroom. It does wonders.

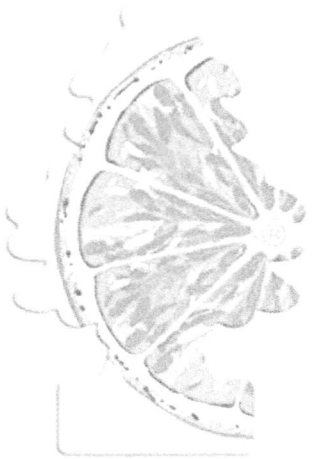

5. **Inflatable bathtub**. No bathtub, no problem. If traveling with an infant or small child, bath time can be troublesome if they can't tolerate a shower. When my children were small, I brought a very small inflatable swimming pool and put it in the shower. They loved it. In today's market, they make inflatable bathtubs. Not only are these great for baths, but when you go on excursions, you can take it and becomes a play area for your child.

Cruising Tips & Hacks from a Professional Cruise Addict

View from aft balcony. The wave created is called a spine.

Belize from aft balcony Thanksgiving cruise 2013.

Must Haves for Cruising During Covid

When COVID-19 hit and cruise ships stopped operating, it was because of the virus. We must be mindful of this and always take precautions, such as regularly washing our hands, and before all meals. Here is what I consider as the germaphobe-friendly travel must-haves for cruising.

1. **Hand sanitizer.** Bring hand sanitizer that clips onto your beach bag. Also, have one that clips to your belt loop or fits inside your pocket. Although all cruise ships have hand sanitizer stations, I like the convenience of always having mine with me.

2. **Sanitizer disinfection wipes.** These are very handy to keep in your purse or beach bag for any occasion, especially on a cruise.

3. **Antiviral surgical masks**. Always wear your facial mask in the public indoor spaces and on the elevators when required. As the distance between the Pandemic started and now, mask requirements are more lenient. I still like to take the safety route.

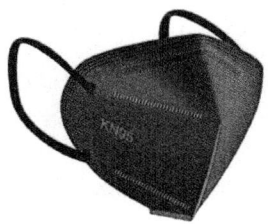

4. **Screen wipes.** For added protection, bring antibacterial screen wipes, and wipe down all doorknobs, drawer pulls, the safe, the telephone, etc., for an added layer of protection in your cabin. Also, frequently wipe down your cell phone, camera, tablets, laptops, and IPAD.

5. **Sanitizer station.** You might purchase a toothbrush sanitizer to store your toothbrush in to keep in sanity.

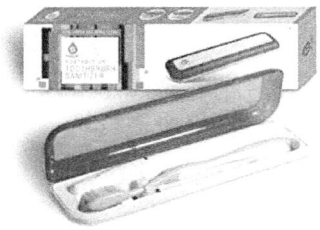

6. **Lysol to Go**. The little spray bottles of Lysol come in handy. They don't take up much room and you can spray it on your cabin door, door handles, sink, toilet, and it kills bacteria, rhinovirus, flu germs, and the norovirus. I usually bring a one-ounce bottle and it lasts all cruise.

7. **Personal water bottle.** Bottled water is available on a cruise but can get expensive. For me, I don't like drinking their tap water, so now what? I solved that problem by bringing along a water bottle with a built-in filtration system. I also bring it when I go on excursions. They can be purchased from Amazon starting at $12.99 up to $60 depending on your budget.

8. **Cell phone sanitizer.** You will use your phone on a cruise. Years ago, you would receive your daily activities printed. Not anymore since they have hired an environment specialist for each ship. Everything now is done through the cruise line's phone app. You will want to keep you phone sanitized each night by using a UV phone sanitizer.

9. Portable safe or diversion bottle for keeping valuables safe while at the pool or on the beach. I have two kinds. One is a safe that attaches to my chair, and the other is what I call a diversion bottle that safely hides my things in them.

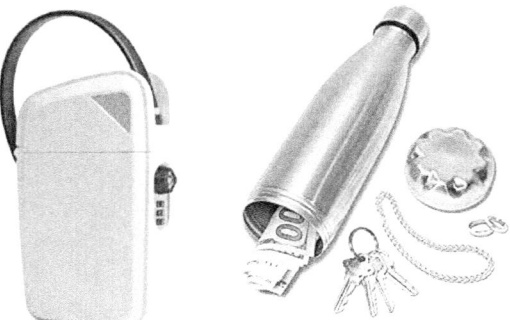

10. **Fiber towel.** I know I said you didn't need to bring a beach towel with you on a cruise because they will supply one for your usage. However, they can be heavy, especially when wet after an excursion or a dip in the ocean. Therefore, I bring a fiber towel with me that is very lightweight, repels sand, and dries extremely fast.

11. **Reef friendly sunscreen.** We always must be aware of our actions on our environment and nature. This is especially

important when snorkeling, diving, or playing in the ocean. Most cruise ships offer reef friendly sunscreen at a very affordable price that if you pre-order will be delivered to your stateroom. You can also search Amazon for reef friendly sunscreen.

12. **Waterproof pouch.** Cruising means you will be around water – the pool, hot tub, beach, boats, and ocean. You will want to protect your cell phone and identification. It is essential that you obtain a waterproof pouch or cellphone holder.

13. **Cable lock.** When you lie around the pool or on a beach, take extra precautions of not getting your personal items stolen. Besides the portable safe I mentioned above, I use a cable

lock and put it around the handles of my beach bag and secure it to the chair. That way it can't be easily grabbed.

14. **Collapsible straws.** One of the best environmental moves I have witnessed since cruising is the elimination of paper and plastic straws and those little paper drink umbrellas. They did nothing but clog the ocean. Today's cruise ships don't use them anymore. So, if you want a straw, I use a collapsible stainless-steel straw that also comes with a case that can attach to your beach bag, purse, belt loop, and many other convenient places.

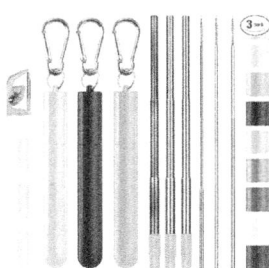

15. **Sunscreen umbrella.** When I took my husband on a New Year's Eve Cruise, he couldn't understand why I brought a compact sunscreen umbrella and kept it in my beach bag. The fact is, I travel nowhere without one. On cruises, sometimes you want a little shade, and none is around. These are perfect, especially the ones that fold upwards as if the wind blows them, they don't break. While on excursions, you will

also need shade whether walking the long cruise terminal to port, or on the beach and you need sun protection. Again, these are perfect. Oh, it also does rain in paradise. I prefer the compact umbrellas with SPF sunscreen built into the material. I never burn, and I have my shade wherever I go.

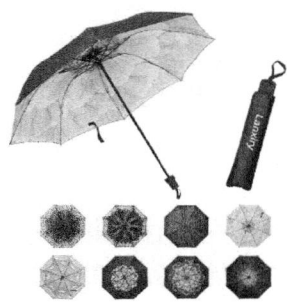

16. Power solar charger for phone. Face it. We live in an electronic world, and you don't escape that by going a cruise. I always pack a solar charger for my phone and my Bluetooth speaker. The best part is as you play, the sun charges the charger and you never run out of a battery charge during an excursion or by the pool.

17. **Cruise power strip/cord.** Cruise ships usually only have one outlet for you to plug in everything you bring. I always bring my computer, cell phone, and Bluetooth speakers for my room and never have an outlet, so I bring my own. Warning!

Make sure whatever you bring is cruise ship approved or it will be confiscated. Also, when you leave your stateroom, unplug all electronics to avoid a fire hazard. I like the ones that also has the USB plug so I can charge my phone too.

18. **Luggage tag holders.** These holders are a bit different than your normal luggage tags. The ones I am referring to hold the tags that for that cruise to identify your cabin. When you go on as many cruises as I do, it is very convenient for me to use these by replacing each content as I cruise.

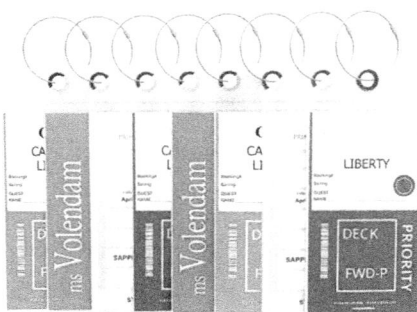

19. **Beach chair clips to secure towels.** The wind can be fierce while cruising and the last thing you need is to chase down a beach towel that flew off. With these cute towel clips, they keep your towel secured to the chair. Hint: I also use these to clamp down my cover up.

20. **First aid kit.** Accidents happen on cruise ships and excursions, and medical supplies aren't readily available. I always pack a mini first-aid kit and keep it in my beach bag.

21. **Medicine emergency kit.** This is something I put together that has over-the-counter medicine that I might need. Items I pack and keep handy include anti-gas pills, diarrhea meds, cough, sinus, aspirin, emergency hydration powder, etc. I pack mine in a gallon Ziplock bag.

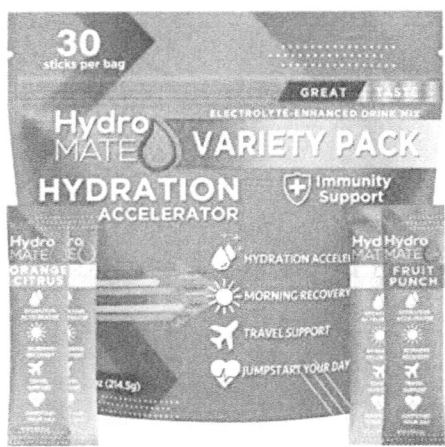

22. **Cruise lanyard.** Once you board the cruise ship, you don't need money or your wallet. Everything is done through your ship's card. Lanyards are especially important because you can hang your card around your neck and forget about it. All cruise ships sell them on board, or you can purchase them before you go. I also bring rhinestone lanyards in the colors to match my evening attire.

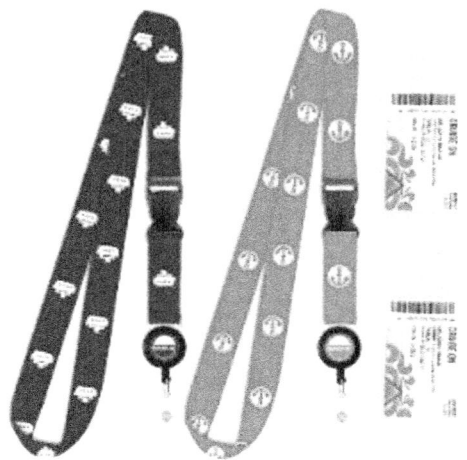

Cruising Tips & Hacks from a Professional Cruise Addict

One of the fun things I do is put my collector pins on my lanyard. This was on the Carnival Vista in August 2021. The first cruise after the Pandemic.

23. **Cellphone lanyard.** This is the greatest invention of all. I love this and use one every day, not just on a cruise to keep up with my phone. I highly recommend them.

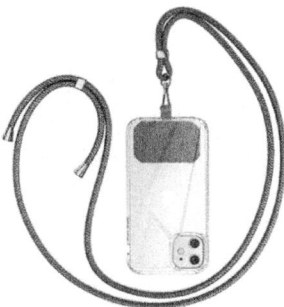

24. **Battery operated portable fan.** Staterooms can become a bit stuffy especially if you are in an interior room. I always bring my battery-operated fan. Why battery operated? I also like

to take mine on excursions, to the pool's cabana, and sometimes to the restaurant on board because it gets hot. I love the fact that the one I have clips to my chair, and it also has a light included to use in the cabin.

25. **Folding storage cubes.** Keeping your things organized can be cumbersome in a cruise cabin. Face it, there isn't much storage and things get tossed around. I always pack a foldable storage cube that way I can keep all of my items in one place. When traveling with others, everyone should use a different color cube for their personal belongings. It makes life so much easier frees the counter space of clutter. They are very convenient and don't take up much space as they fold flat.

26. **Rubber beach tote.** I love the Bogg Beach Tote because it is waterproof and washes very easy. It comes in a variety of sizes and colors to fit your needs.

Cruise Tip Hack: If you use an umbrella, if you put the handle inside the bag, you can secure it to the Bogg tote bag with a small bungee cord to the handle and it won't fly away, and you won't have to hold it. I also use a towel clip to clip it to the tote bag as added security.

Dr. Mel on aft deck of the Carnival Valor, November 2021, practicing what she preaches -- the fan keeping her cool, the umbrella protecting her from the sun, the tumbler keeping her drink ice cold. "I'm living my best life on a cruise ship one month at a time." Dr. Mel

Decorating Your Cabin and/or Your Door

I love decorating my cabin and my cabin door. If my sisters and I have something special going on, like a birthday, or a holiday, we decorate according to that theme. Instead of using tape, etc., we use magnetic hooks to hang things on the walls or from the ceiling. We also decorate our cabin doors with magnetic signs, banners, plaques, etc. This always makes it easier to find your cabin among the others.

There is caution when decorating your stateroom or cabin door. Never nail anything or use tape because you can damage the surface. You don't need that added expense. Take a look at some of my decorations I use for our cabins. You can find inspiration anywhere and purchase many magnetic signs from Amazon. The goal, be creative and have fun.

Cruise Tip Hack: Take a white board and dry erasers and hang on the outside of the cabin. This is always a way to leave messages, but your fellow passengers often do too.

Cruise Tip Hack: Visit the Dollar Store, Dollar Tree, or Dollar General to purchase many door decorations. It is easy to make them yourself.

If you are an art lover, don't miss the art display and auctions.

Dr. Mel on the aft balcony on her 64th birthday, March 2022, on the Carnival Valor.

Packing Your Bags

Dr. Mel in 2003 on the Carnival Conquest during formal night in the main dining room.

For some, packing is the most stressing thing they do before going on a cruise. Maybe that is why I stay packed. However, with careful planning and thinking through your wardrobe, you won't over pack and will have the necessary clothing you want. Here are my tips and suggestions when it comes to packing. Coordinate your outfits. Bring clothing that you can mix and match. You can use the same pair of pants, with a different shirt or jacket to change it up. I like to plan my colors that I wear so that no matter what I grab, it will match something else I brought.

Besides formal night, often cruises will have specialty fun nights that you will want an outfit to go along with the theme. Most cruises will have an 80s, Rock and Roll, or Motown night. Other cruises have White Night, where everyone wears white. I will bring an outfit to wear befitting the theme. Also, themed party cruises offer many opportunities to dress to impress. I love the *Star Trek* cruise and being able to become a Vulcan. This year alone, I have attended a Halloween Cruise where one night we all costumed it up, New Year's Eve Party where I dressed in the Roaring Twenties, a Mardi Gras Party where I brought my colorful Mardi Gras jogging suit and a fancy Mardi Gras hat, beads, and boa, and Easter, where I wore my best Easter dress. To find out if there are any special events on the ship during your cruise, contact the cruise line and ask. With all of that said, dress codes are basically the same on all ships, and with planning, you will have everything you need.

Dr. Mel dressed for the 1920s Roaring Twenties Party on the Royal Princess May 2018.

Dress Code

Mostly, shipboard dress is casual during the day. That means you can wear shorts, jeans, T-shirts, tank tops, rompers, etc. When on the Lido deck, swimming area, you can wear your bathing suit, but if you go into the eating areas, you will need to wear a cover up of some sort, so always have one with you. Most three to five-day cruises will have one formal night, and those above six will have two: so, plan accordingly. Formal wear for men includes dark suits or tuxedos and for women a formal gown or cocktail dress. The rest of the evenings are informal.

Cruise Tip Hack: Always take a picture of your luggage. That way, if they are lost, you can show guest services exactly what your luggage looks like.

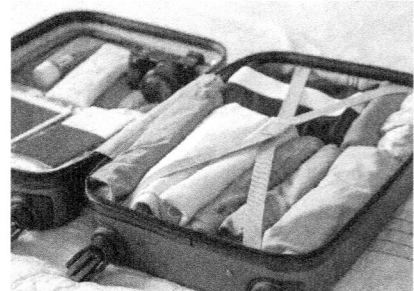

Cruise Tip Hack: To save packing space, roll your clothes. Also, I have used the bags that are vacuum tight and takes the air out. Most nowadays come with a pump for added value and convenience.

Dr. Mel in front of the Carnival Valor in October 2021. Her aft room was just above the L in Carnival.

Traveling with Children

Cruising with children is fun and a great way to explore the world and introduce them to new cultures. Most cruise ships are floating resorts filled with activities for children to keep them entertained. I will never forget my very first cruise with one of my children. At the time, she was five, and I was five months pregnant. I'll always cherish this trip as well as the others that I've taken with my children. Most recently, I had the pleasure of cruising with two of my grandchildren. I must admit, it was one of the most fun cruises I have ever taken. To see the awe and wonderment in their eyes brought so much joy that I can't even explain it.

Dr. Mel with her daughter, Erin, age 6, in 1984. Dr. Mel was five months pregnant with her daughter Kelly at the time.

Cruising Tips & Hacks from a Professional Cruise Addict

Dr. Mel, five months pregnant, pictured with daughter Erin in 1984 on the Royal Caribbean cruise excursion. This was Erin's first cruise and, as of today, hasn't been back on one.

Dr. Mel, pregnant with Kelly, in 1984 in St. Andres.

Dr. Mel, Kelly (age 11 and the one she was pregnant with in the last picture), Mike, and Jamie (age 6) on a family cruise, 1996. Note: The grandkids on the next page are the children of Kelly, pictured in the middle. Oh, how times flies when you cruise.

Dr. Mel, present day, with her grandchildren, Roger and Blythe, on the beach in Cozumel, June 2022. This was the first cruise for the grandchildren. They are now cruise addicts and I feel as if I have come full circle.

However, you still need to plan and be prepared to ensure smooth sailing when traveling with children. Here is what you need to know.

Seek Kid Friendly Activities

There are plenty of activities aboard a cruise ship for children, including miniature golf, shuffleboard, ping-pong, video games, an arcade, water slide, beanbag toss, basketball, volleyball, and Build a Bear. Of course, cruise ships also offer a day camp and lots of activities, including arts and crafts and board games.

Cruise Tip Hack: Register your children into the Kid's Camp prior to boarding to reserve their spot. If they decide to attend, they can, but it is still an option for them not to.

Roger and Blythe having fun in the arcade on a virtual reality ride on the Carnival Valor June 2022.

Cruising Tips & Hacks from a Professional Cruise Addict

Blythe and Roger playing shuffleboard on the first day of their very first cruise, June 2022.

Blythe and Roger having a great time in the video arcade on the ship Valor in June 2022.

Roger and Blythe enjoying the water slide and pool on the Valor, June 2022.

Port Excursions with Children

Port excursions offer a wonderful opportunity for children to learn about other cultures and sightseeing. Depending on the country, there are many historical tourism spots you can introduce your children to. From Mayan ruins to castles to experiencing local cuisine, there is plenty for your family to do. I recommend you book your excursions through the cruise line to make sure that they are kid friendly and bring extra cash for the taxi fares and tips. This also helps to ensure that they remain safe. My grandchildren loved the beach excursions that included the watersport activities, especially snorkeling.

Heading back on board the Valor after a day of sightseeing, snorkeling, and shopping.

Blythe and Roger playing in the sand in Progresso.

Blythe after seeing her first fish snorkeling in Cozumel and Roger soaking in the sun. They loved their day at the beach in Cozumel.

To make your child's or grandchild's cruise a pleasant experience, I recommend the following.

1. Teach each child their full name, first, middle, and last name, their date of birth, including the year they were born, their address, and phone number. Upon boarding and disembarking a ship, nine times out of ten, the security member in charge will ask them these questions. They will also ask them how they are related to you. So be prepared!

   Cruise Hack Tip: Practice with your child before going on the cruise because being asked by a Custom official in full uniform can intimidate your child. Explain to them, they are asking for their safety.

2. Bring all your over-the-counter medicines your child might need, including allergy medication, cough medicine, and fever reducer. You never know when you might need it. I also bring a thermometer and all prescription medications.

   Cruise Hack Tip: For children allergic to bees, make certain to carry the EpiPen and keep it handy.

3. Bring a stroller for the boat and for excursions. Make sure it has a shade and a portable fan because it can get very hot.

4. Bring your child a cup and keep it filled with water and keep them hydrated. Also, make use of the free drinks on the Lido deck that includes tea and lemonade. The sun takes a lot out of you, and it is extremely important to keep children hydrated.

Blythe staying hydrated after swimming and sliding down the waterslide.

5. If your child is not potty trained, bring disposable swimming diapers for them, as they are not supplied on the ship.

6. Use lots of safe sunscreen, SPF 50 Sport/Waterproof, made for children every time they go into the sun. Apply the sunscreen while in your cabin, and then again, every thirty minutes or after each time in the water to avoid sunburns.

Dr. Mel's grandchildren, Roger and Blythe, sunscreened up before going into ocean.

Cruise Hack Tip: Provide each child with their own sunscreen, sunscreen lip balm, and beach bag and teach them the responsibility of keeping sunscreened up. Of course, you will need to supervise.

Cruise Hack Tip: My grandchildren loved having their own umbrella around the pool on deck and on excursions to get out of the sun when they needed to.

Here is my granddaughter, Blythe, at the pool under her umbrella and the battery-operated fan to keep cool.

7. I highly recommend that each child has a pair of sunglasses. The sun is very bright.

   Cruise Hack Tip: Children also like using swim goggles. It's best not to purchase the cheap ones as they tend to fall apart.

8. Children will need to have their birth certificates or a passport when boarding the ship or debarking the ship at ports.

   Cruise Hack Tip: Keep the important documents in a Ziplock bag to prevent them from getting wet.

9. Investigate babysitting options provided on board. Most cruise lines have the Kids Ocean Club for the day but for children over two and often offer one night of babysitting. Other lines have babysitters on board that you can hire. You will need to inquire at the service desk or call before you get on the ship.

On the left, Dr. Mel with Roger and Blythe. On the right, Dr. Mel with Roger, Blythe took this picture. Oh, I not once put them in the Ocean Club as we had so much fun being together.

10. Encourage your child to bring a small duffle bag with their toys or games they want to play with as none are provided on the ship. This includes a sand bucket and shovel for the beach excursions.

11. Bring a book or two for rainy day reading or for you to read to them before they go to bed. If you don't know what activities or games to bring, you may always choose my coloring and activity books for kids.

AVAILABLE ON AMAZON.COM

12. Involve your kids in planning for the daily activities. There are plenty of things for the family to do together, such as miniature golf and board games. Three of my grandchildren's

favorite activities were the feature length movie on the Lido deck with popcorn, Bingo, and the Build A Bear workshop.

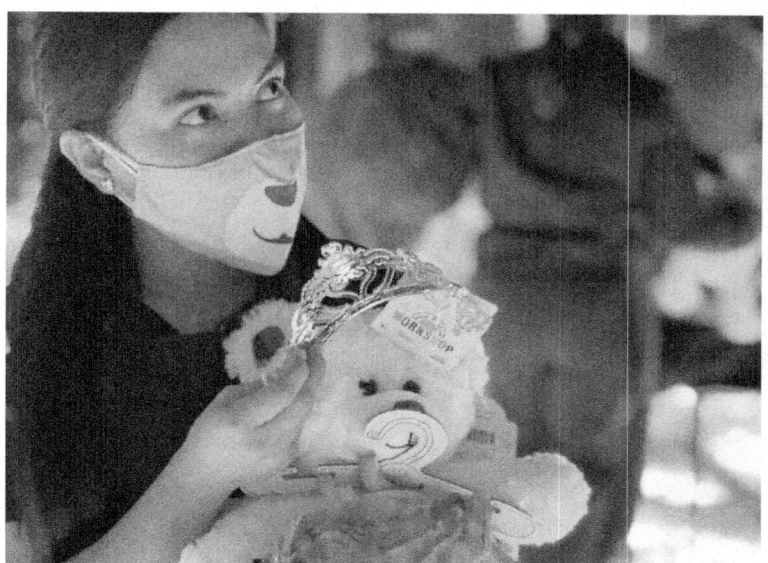

My grandchildren had a blast picking out which bear and clothes for their Bear.

Cruise Tip Hack: Sign up early for the Build A Bear workshop as the spots fill up fast, and if you are at the end, it can be a very long wait.

13. If your child can't swim, I recommend you bring a life jacket or toddler puddle jumpers that are Coast Guard approved. There are several kinds to choose from, including life vests, half vests with the floatation bands on that go on the arms, or one piece. On the Lido deck, pain pool area on the ship, they also offer life jackets.

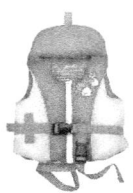  

Cruise Etiquette

Teach your children cruise safety and etiquette. Please and thank you go a long way with the cruise staff. The best rules to teach them are:

1. Don't run, walk, push, or shove others.
2. Use your inside voice, always.
3. Use manners, always. Remember, please and thank you goes a long way.
4. Always let the people come out of the elevator prior to entering.
5. Don't push all the elevator buttons.
6. Dry off before sitting on any furniture.
7. Be quiet in the halls not to disturb other passengers.
8. Don't climb on the railing.
9. Don't touch the artwork displayed throughout the ship.
10. Don't splash others in any of the pools or hot tubs.
11. Wait your turn for the super slide, at the buffet and the ice cream dispensary.

12. Never, ever pee in the pool or hot tub.
13. Remember, it is the journey and not the destination. Make memories and start traditions.
14. If you find a duck, take care of it or rehide it for others.

Cruise Tip Hack: Starting traditions on cruises is so much fun. One that my family started was taking a picture in front of an Elvis or Marilyn Monroe statue in Cozumel. We are now six generations strong posing in front of them.

Dr. Mel on the left in 2015 and her grandchildren in 2022 posing in front of the same statue.

Ducks on Board

Besides the games and activities, you bring from home, there are many other creative ways to keep your child entertained. All cruise ships have a library with books you can borrow and plenty of board games. This is a perfect area for a rainy day or if you need time to get away from the sun, so take advantage.

Some cruise ship passengers hide ducks and place them around the ship for children to find, so if you see one, it's yours to take or you can hide them again for others to find. Children get a big kick finding the ducks.

Kelly, Dr. Mel's middle daughter, found a duck on the Carnival Valor ship, May 2022. Yes, we hid it for others to find.

Sometimes you find a duck hiding in plain sight.

Cruise Hack Tip: Some people create tags and attach them to the ducks. Tags are easy to create in a Microsoft Word document or a label maker. You can also purchase them on Amazon. Here is one of my tags I created that I attach with a ribbon. I have received pictures from people from all over the world and some of my ducks end up on other cruise ships.

Cruise Hack Tip: Some cruises do a gift exchange. How does this work? Find a group on Facebook for the ship you are sailing and the date. They are often created to exchange either a small gift at the beginning of the cruise or one every day. Items I have been gifted with include sunscreen, sunhat, a magic wand, a lanyard, a waterproof pouch, a collapsible straw, a small spray bottle with a battery-operated fan, and a small foldable ice chest. My favorite was a small lapel pin for my lanyard from the ship I was sailing on before I became eligible to receive them. A gift exchange can be a lot of fun.

Cruise Hack Tip: An alternative to hiding ducks includes hiding Easter eggs during that season. I purchase the cardboard ones and hand-painted them and hid around the ship. At Christmas, I hid little a Santa Claus, elves, and ribbons with a jingle bell on them.

Here are several of the hand-painted eggs I did using Sharpie markers. These are cardboard and proved to be a lot of fun.

Creating a Privacy Area for Kids in the Cabin

Face it, cruise cabins are small and sometimes there will be four people in the cabin. Oh, boy! It is essential that everyone in the cabin keep their area clean and clutter free, so make use of the closets, drawers, and put suitcases, etc., beneath the bed.

Cruise Hack Tip: To create a private barrier in a small cabin using the pull-down bed, you can create a privacy barrier by using either a black out curtain or a lightweight microfiber beach towel. It's easy to assemble by using the magnetic hooks. To create the barrier, use the magnetic hooks to attach the microfiber beach towel to the ceiling. Kids love it because they have a dedicated place to call their own and it gives everyone privacy.

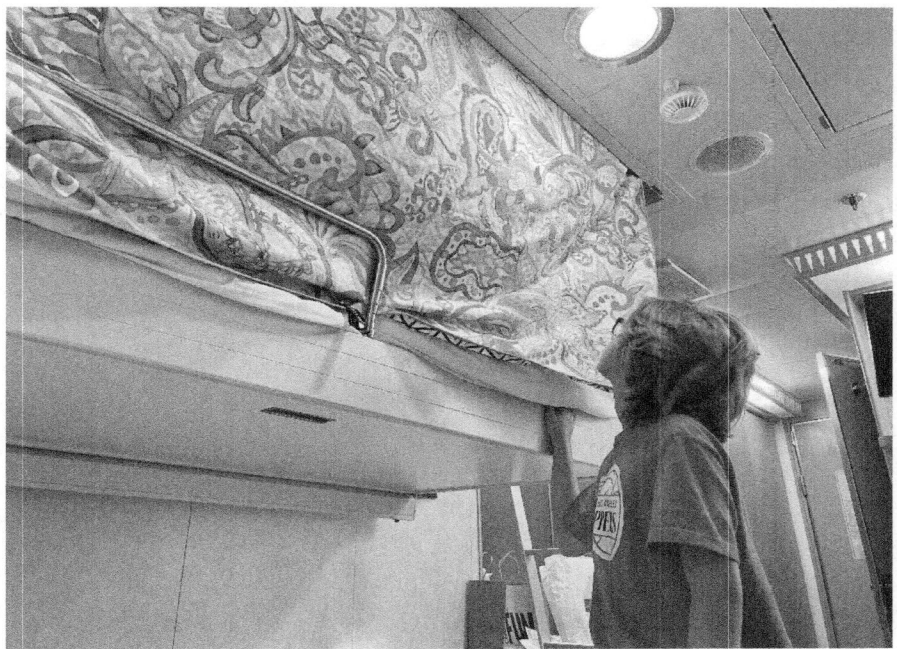

The microfiber beach towel hung with magnetic hooks, creating privacy for all. Roger checking on his little sister hidden away behind the privacy curtain.

Cruise Hack Tip: For added comfort, when I created the privacy wall above, I also hung a small battery-operated fan to the ceiling with a magnetic hook to create airflow. The fan also had a built-in night light.

Best Cruise Lines for Kids

Spencer Brown of Cruise Critic says, "Certain cruise lines are better for kids of different ages." She recommends Cunard for babies and toddlers, Disney for children under 10, Carnival for children and tweens, and Royal Caribbean for teens. The main dining room offered lots of fun entertainment, including the nightly "Showtime." My grandchildren loved the magician who came to our table at breakfast and at dinner and performed magic card tricks.

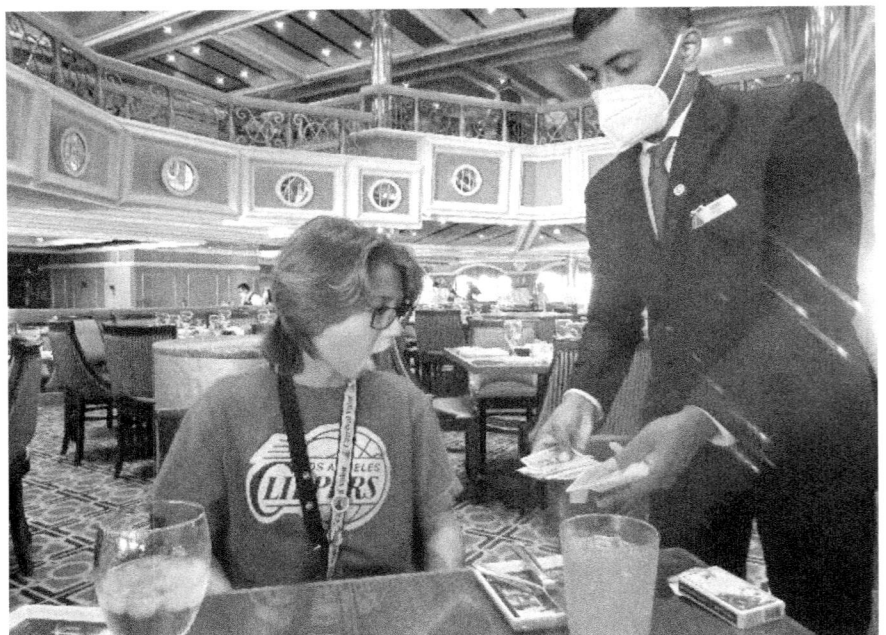

Roger, Dr. Mel's grandson, having fun with the magician performing magic tricks.

Cunard – a luxury cruise line offering childcare at 1 year+ and special splash areas for diapered children on some ships. This is a great ship to travel with toddlers.

Disney Cruise Line – Disney-themed ships bring the magic of Disney on a cruise with activities for children of all ages. They have water slides and splash areas and cater to shore excursions for children.

Bonus: privacy curtains between children's area of stateroom and parents' bed.

Carnival Cruise Line – Carnival is one of my favorite cruise lines for family fun. There is always something to do for children and lots of family activities. The price for a Carnival cruise can't be beat as they are affordable. Teens and Tweens love cruising on the Carnival Cruise Line.

Dr. Mel's grandchildren watching the sail away from New Orleans on the Valor.

Royal Caribbean – Great option for teens with extensive at sea entertainment and clubs. Private stateroom babysitting is available for a fee. Some ships offer group childcare as young as 6 months and/or splash areas for babies and toddlers.

Picture of the balcony on the Carnival Glory.

Cruising Tips & Hacks from a Professional Cruise Addict

Dr. Mel having a great time at the piano bar on the Ecstasy, February 2022.

A little hide-away in Costa Maya.

Excursions

Another lazy day at the beach in Roatan Honduras.

While being on a cruise ship is like staying at a resort on water, once you arrive at port, you'll want to see the port and engage in the local activities. I highly recommend that first time cruises book their shore excursions through the cruise ship. Why? The major benefit is that when you book through the cruise line, you are guaranteed your return to the ship on time. Trust me, if you don't make it back to the ship on time, it will leave without you. Now, if you are delayed on an excursion booked through the cruise line, they will notify the ship and the ship will wait for you. That's a tremendous bonus, don't you think?

So, what excursions should you book? That answer is as tall as it is long – it depends on your interest and level of expertise. For instance, if you're a certified diver, you can go on an excursion with divers at your level. However, if you're not certified, you'll be guided to a snorkeling excursion. Again, it depends on your level of expertise and interest.

For me, I have been on so many cruises I know where I want to go when I get off the ship and usually take a cab. However, I am a very experienced cruiser and know my way around. I still recommend that you book any excursion through the ship and stay safe.

Dr. Mel enjoying a day at the beach in Costa Maya.

Cruise Hack: Avoid renting scooters, motorcycles, golf carts, and cars while on an excursion. You could find yourself in a heap of trouble.

Dr. Mel on a snorkeling excursion in Jamaica in 2017.

Beverages Packages

Earlier, I mentioned that everything on a cruise is taken care of for you except for adult beverages and/or soda packages on board. Those are an additional cost. I always purchase the beverage package before I leave for the cruise for my adult beverages. When I do, I save up to 10% and during the

cruise; and I don't get charged additional for those drinks. The average cost per day, pre-cruise pricing, for this package is $51.95 a day. In the long run, it is far cheaper to purchase the package verses buying individual cocktails and specialty coffee. The average price of a specialty coffee is $6.75 per cup and for wine around $12.50 per glass. Martinis and other cocktails can cost up to $15.00 per drink. The beverage package comes with a 15-drink maximum per day, which is plenty. Therefore, in the long run, I have found that it is less expensive to purchase the package than not. On the Carnival Cruise Line, this package is called the Cheers Package.

Included in the Cheers Package

Up to 15 Alcoholic Beverages per day ($20 or less drinks)
Bottled Water *(About $2 per bottle individually)*
Soda *($2.25 if purchased individually)*

Cruising Tips & Hacks from a Professional Cruise Addict

Milk Shakes ($4 if purchased individually)
Specialty Coffee *($1-$6 depending how fancy you are)*
Energy Drinks *($4.95 if purchased individually)*
Coconut Water, Vitamin Water and Powerade
Smoothies *($5.50 if purchased individually)*

TROPICAL CLASSICS:

9.25

Enjoy these classic favorites with a Carnival twist!
Prepared with two pours of our finest liquors.

MARGARITA
The perfect blend of El Jimador Tequila, Patrón Citrónge and lime juice. It doesn't get tastier than this.

Upgrade to Patrón Silver for just $2.00 extra.

TEQUILA SUNRISE
Herradura Silver Tequila, Orange Juice, finished with Grenadine. Nobody does it better.

BAHAMA MAMA
Flor de Caña Rum, Malibu Coconut Rum, grenadine, pineapple and orange juice. A perfect drink for relaxing at sea.

MAI TAI
A tropical tradition that blends Bacardi Rum, Bacardi 8 Rum, Orange Curaçao, orgeat syrup and limes.

RUM AND GINGER BEER
A spicy yet refreshing blend of Brugal Añejo Rum, Ginger Beer and fresh lime juice.

SEX ON THE BEACH
A delicious, fruity mix of Absolut Vodka, Peach Schnapps, orange juice and cranberry juice.

THE CRUISER
Chill and enjoy this perfect complement to any cruise. A blend of Absolut Vodka, Malibu Coconut Rum and Peach Schnapps, mixed with pineapple, cranberry and orange juice.

PIRATE PUNCH
Bacardi Rum, Bacardi 8, Disaronno Amaretto, cranberry, pineapple and orange juice.

Tina, Dr. Mel's best friend, enjoying an adult beverage as part of the Cheers package on the Carnival Ecstasy.

So, if you're trying to determine whether a drink package is worth it, you must determine how much you plan to or want to drink. For me, I always start my morning with a fresh specialty coffee, at least two. Then I'll move to either Mimosas or a Bloody Mary with breakfast. That means before I even make it to the pool, I have had at least four drinks out of my fifteen. By the time I spend a couple of hours at the pool, that's about three or four more drinks. Then, dinner and the nightly entertainment and I want a glass of wine with my meal and at the show and comedy club. Therefore, having the drink package is worth it.

Consider the following when making your determination for the drink package.

You have to purchase the drink package for the entire cruise and not just for a single day and all adults in the same cabin must purchase.

Dr. Mel and Tina enjoying a drink at the Neon Bar before the comedy show.

All adults in the same cabin must purchase a drink package if one does.

You may bring one 750 ml or less bottle of wine or champagne per person on board or one 12 pack of soda/energy drinks.

You can purchase a bottle of alcohol from the cruise line before you sail and have it delivered to your room or the moment you arrive, ask your cabin steward to order it.

BEERS
FROTHY AND REFRESHING. MUCH LIKE THE SEA ON A WINDY DAY.

Domestic 16 oz.
Bud Light Lime 6.25
Bud Light 6.25
Budweiser 6.25
Michelob Ultra 6.25
Miller Lite 6.25
Coors Light 6.25

Craft
Sam Adams, Boston Lager, *16 oz.* 6.50
Sam Adams, Rebel IPA, *16 oz.* 6.50
Coney Island, Mermaid, Pilsner, *16 oz.* 6.50
Angel City Brewery, IPA, *16 oz.* 6.50
Blue Moon, Belgium White, *16 oz.* 6.50
Sierra Nevada, Pale Ale, *16 oz.* 6.50
Saltwater Brewery, Sea Cow Stout 6.25
Estrella Daura, Gluten Free 6.25

(Ask about our selection of local craft beers)

Imported
Foster's Lager, *750 ml.* 7.95
Heineken, *16 oz.* 6.50
Heineken Light, *16 oz.* 6.50
Pilsner Urquell, *16 oz.* 6.50
Corona 5.75
Corona Light 5.75
Dos Equis 5.75

Adult Beverage
Mike's Hard Lemonade 6.25

Cider 16 oz.
Angry Orchard 6.50

Zero-Proof
Buckler 5.75

Cruising Tips & Hacks from a Professional Cruise Addict

CHAMPAGNES & WINES
WHEN IN DOUBT, TOAST TO GOOD COMPANY. THAT'S HOW THE CLASSY FOLKS DO IT.

	GL	BTL
Sparkling Wine		
Domaine Chandon, 'Brut', *California*	9.75	37.00
Rosé, Domaine Ste. Michelle 'Brut', *Washington*	10.00	38.00
White Wines		
Pinot Grigio, *Ecco Domani, Italy*	10.25	39.00
Sauvignon Blanc, *Santa Helena, Chile*	7.25	27.00
Sauvignon Blanc, *Oyster Bay, New Zealand*	9.25	35.00
Chardonnay, *Santa Helena, Chile*	7.00	26.00
Chardonnay, *Kendall-Jackson 'Vintner's Reserve', California*	10.00	38.00
Sweet, Blush & Rosé		
Lambrusco, *Reunite, Italy*	7.50	28.00
White Zinfandel, *Barefoot, California*	7.50	28.00
Moscato, *Castello del Poggio, Italy*	10.00	38.00
Pinot Noir Rosé, *'GIFFT' by Kathie Lee Gifford, California*	7.75	29.00
Riesling, *Chateau Ste. Michelle, Washington*	8.00	30.00
White Blend, *Conundrum, California*	12.75	49.00
Red Wines		
Pinot Noir, *Castle Rock, California*	8.75	33.00
Pinot Noir, *Layer Cake, California*	10.50	40.00
Merlot, *Santa Helena, Chile*	7.25	27.00
Merlot, *Columbia Crest, Washington*	10.25	39.00
Cabernet Sauvignon, *Santa Helena, Chile*	7.00	26.00
Cabernet Sauvignon, *Layer Cake, California*	10.00	38.00
Red Blend, *'GIFFT' by Kathie Lee Gifford, California*	8.50	32.00
Shiraz, *Peter Lehman 'Portrait', Australia*	10.00	38.00

For kids, or for adults who what soft drinks, they have a Bubble Package.

ICY INVENTIONS — 8.50
MITTENS RECOMMENDED. WHAT, YOU DIDN'T PACK MITTENS? UH-OH.

Kiss on the Lips
We've mixed up some mango purée with Peach Schnapps and a splash of grenadine, just for you. How romantic!

Mocha Chocolate Getaway
A mix of Irish Cream, Flor de Caña Rum, and rich Ghirardelli chocolate. Seriously, sinfully delicious.

Hurricane Wave
Layers of hurricane and banana daiquiri crafted with Bacardi Rum. Is it windy in here or is it just us?

Daiquiris
Choose from Piña Colada, Strawberry, Banana, Peach, Raspberry, Mango, Lemonade or Hurricane.

Add a floater of Bacardi Oakheart Spiced Rum for $2.00.
All these great drinks are available zero-proof for $5.50.

SMOOTHIES & KIDS' FAVES — 5.50
KIDS LOVE SMOOTHIES. ADULTS LOVE SMOOTHIES. SEAGULLS, HOWEVER, PREFER FRENCH FRIES.

Peach Strawberry Combo.
Now kids won't have to pick a favorite. Because we've layered this fruity, frothy drink with both peaches and strawberries. Talk about a dreamy combo.

Strawberry Piña Colada
We've taken the classic Piña Colada and made it kid-friendly with a splash of strawberry and a couple of whirls in our smoothie machine.

Mango Madness
Our idea of a tropical taste treat. Amp up the fun and go exotic with this sweet and refreshing combination of mango and grenadine.

Banana Split
Our spin on this summer dessert – banana stirred into delicious chocolate milk made with Hershey's Syrup.

Dr. Mel with her sister Caylen at the Captain's Party on the Royal Princess in 2018. We were front and center pouring the champagne into one glass allowing it to fill the rest of the glasses. I rare moment.

Specialty Dining

Although all meals are free in the main dining room and other areas on the ship, including the buffet, most cruise ships offer the specialty dining rooms. You have several choices, but my favorite is the Steak House and the Chef's Table. Both are five-star culinary experiences. After you book your cruise, check out their specialty dining restaurants and book in advance of your departure. Not only will you save money, but you can choose your time and date. Often, once on board, these are sold-out.

Our steak comped dinner. Thank you, Carnival.

Last night on the Glory, February 2022, in the main dining room as the stcff sang.

Bonus Cruise Packing Hacks

I have learned many cruise hacks in during my travels. Listed below are the ones that are important to know before you go.

1. When packing, don't pack everything you need into one suitcase. If it is lost, you won't have anything. I have only lost my luggage one time during a cruise, but it was a nightmare. My luggage with all of my sleep attire, bathing suits, and casual wear never made it on board while my other suitcase did. In hindsight, I now pack in two suitcases and put a variety in each. That way, if one is lost, I still have the basics. The same can be applied when traveling with a companion. Divide and conquer by sharing the suitcases and pack in both.
2. Pack extra luggage tags in case one is lost during transit.
3. Pack Ziplock bags of all sizes. They come in handy if you have to carry a wet bathing suit, or to put snacks in for you or your children from the buffet to your room.
4. Pack a nightlight or a flashlight.
5. Pack a small empty duffel bag inside your luggage. That way you can carry home your souvenirs or things that now won't fit in your luggage.
6. Consider a roll-on shopping cart with a seat to use as your carry on. I have one and love it. Anytime I need to sit and rest, I have it with me. Lines during boarding or debarkation can get tiresome.

7. Use air-tight bags to pack to save space.
8. Many people roll their garments when packing to save space and to keep the wrinkles away.
9. Packing cubes come in handy when packing and to keep you organized.

Dr. Mel in Cozumel with the Carnival Ecstasy and Breeze in the background.

What to Do If You Get Sick on a Cruise

Dr. Mel's black eye.

Getting sick or getting an injury is no fun, especially if you're on a cruise vacation. I consider myself extremely lucky because of the number of times I have gone on cruises; I have only gotten sick one time, sinus infection, and injured one time. I slipped, fell, and hit my forehead and eye while going to the bathroom in the middle of the night. This was on the first night of the cruise and spent the rest of the seven-day cruise with a black eye. It was no fun. However, because I was prepared and brought my emergency medical kit, I came out on the upper end of the deal. The key to not getting sick is to follow certain guidelines. Here they are for you.

1. Wash your hands often to avoid getting sick on a cruise. Use lots of soap. Also, always keep with you a travel size bottle of antibacterial gel or wipes to use when water isn't available.
2. On the onset of any illness, notify the cruise ship's medical staff. This is extremely important now that COVID has entered into the arena. You should always report a cough,

vomiting, diarrhea, sore throat, fever, loss of taste, or a loss of smell.
3. Travel with your emergency medical supplies.
4. If the medical staff recommends you quarantine, always follow their rules and guidelines to protect yourself, family, staff, and other cruisers.
5. Follow all mask guidelines in place.
6. If you are prone to seasickness, take Dramamine. Ginger candy and drinking ginger ale are also useful in this situation. Always consult with your physician prior to leaving for a cruise.
7. Don't panic! Knowledge is key here.

Travel Insurance

Most cruise lines offer travel insurance when you book a cruise. Is it necessary? I think so. There are plenty of companies that offer travel insurance besides the cruise line. I opted to purchase a yearly plan with a provider as it was far less than per cruise. Since I vacation on a cruise ship once a month, it is advantageous for me to do so. If a medical emergency surfaces, interrupted flights, cancelled cruise, or if you or your traveling companion cannot cruise, you will be covered. You heard of Murphy's Law, right? My sister, even after I reminded her to get travel insurance, didn't and she had a medial emergency on board. It cost her several hundreds of dollars out of pocket which was four times as much as a yearly plan would have been. Yikes! She found out the hard way. My plan cost me $287 for the year and covers up to $50,000 medical expenses, $100,000 medical transport, and so much more. I strongly advise that you research the companies and purchase the plan that suits your needs and budget.

Before you Go, Girl

I bet you didn't think there was so much to cruising. But wait! I'm not finished. There are several things you need to take care of before you leave for your cruise. Take a look at this list.

1. Print three copies of your boarding pass, and COVID TEST and put one in your carryon, one in your purse, and give one to a traveling companion. That way, if you lose one, you have backups.

2. Print two luggage tags per bag and place one on the top handle and the other on the side handle. Often, tags come off and you don't want to be the person looking for their lost luggage.
3. Contact the post office and have them hold your mail.
4. Stop your newspaper delivery or ask a friend or neighbor to pick up the newspaper each day while you are gone. The last thing you need is for them to pile up, announcing that you are out of town.

Cruising Tips & Hacks from a Professional Cruise Addict

5. Make a copy of your passport and any credit card you may use and put them in a safe place. If you lose them during your trip, you can easily retrieve the information.
6. Call your bank that issued the credit card you will use and inform them you will travel out of the States.
7. Place a business card with your name, address, and telephone number in each of your suitcases. If your luggage tag falls off, the cruise line will still be able to identify your luggage that way.
8. Arrange for someone to take care of your animals each day or arrange for their care in a kennel.
9. Pack a small carryon bag that has one change of clothing, your medications, travel documents, and jewelry.
10. Get change, including $1 bills, to tip the porters who help you onto and off the ship with your luggage.

Dr. Mel on the aft balcony of the Carnival Valor October 2021.

Dr. Mel and her mom on a 2014 Mother's Day Cruise.

Cruising Tips & Hacks from a Professional Cruise Addict

CRUISE PLANNING GUIDE

Cruise Line: _____ **Date of Cruise:** _____
Booking #: _____ **Transportation to Port:** _____
Travel Agent: _____ **Phone:** ( ) _____
Celebration: _____
Traveling Companions: _____
_____
_____
_____

Day 1 Destination: _____

    Excursion: _____

    What to wear during the day: _____

    What to wear during the evening: _____

Day 2 Destination: _____

    Excursion: _____

    What to wear: _____

    What to wear during the evening: _____

Day 3 Destination: _____

Excursion: _____

    What to wear: _____

Day 4 Destination: _____

    Excursion: _____

    What to wear: _____

Day 5 Destination: _____

    Excursion: _____

    What to wear: _____

Day 6 Destination: _____

    Excursion: _____

    What to wear: _____

Day 7 Destination: _____

    Excursion: _____

    What to wear: _____

Notes:

_____
_____
_____
_____
_____
_____
_____
_____

Cruising Tips & Hacks from a Professional Cruise Addict

PACKING CHECKLIST

Cruise Line: _____ Date of Cruise: _____
Booking #: _____ Number of Days: _____
Port: _____ Transportation to Port: _____
Destination: _____
Celebration: _____

ESSENTIALS

- Driver's License
- Money
- Travel Documents
- Credit Cards
- Boarding Pass
- COVID Test Results
- Vaccination Card
- Purse
- Wallet

Toiletries

- Toothbrush
- Toothpaste
- Mouthwash
- Shampoo
- Conditioner
- Deodorant
- Razor
- Shaving Cream
- Sunscreen
- Body Lotion
- Aloe Lotion
- Contact Case
- Lip Balm
- Makeup
- Hair Ties
- Bobby Pins
- Makeup Remover
- Styling Gel
- Hairspray

Beach Clothing

- Bathing Suits
- Cover up
- Flip flops
- Water shoes

Personal Clothing

- Panties
- Bras
- Pajamas
- Socks

Daywear

- 2 Shorts
- 1 Jean
- 2 T-shirts
- 1 Tank Tops

Evening Wear

- 1 Formal Night Attire
- 5 Casual

Outerwear

- Sweater
- Rain Poncho

Shoes

- Tennis Shoes
- Flipflops
- Sandals
- Flats
- Heels

Health and Safety Needs

- First Aid Kit
- OTC Medicines
- Prescription Medicines
- Sunscreen
- Sunglasses
- Allergy Medications
- EpiPen
- Health Insurance Card
- Eyeglasses

Cruising Tips & Hacks from a Professional Cruise Addict

Electronics

- Flashlight
- Computer
- iPad
- Phone
- Bluetooth Speaker
- Sun Charger
- Charging Block
- Cords
- Selfie Stick
- Headphones
- Portable Fan
- Camera

Decorations

- Door Magnets
- Plagues
- Whiteboard
- Streamers

Miscellaneous

- Book to Read
- Waterproof Case for Phone
- Beach Bag
- Beach Towel Clips
- Magnetic Hooks
- Duct Tape
- Umbrella
- Backpack
- Lanyard for Cruise Card
- Lanyard for Phone
- Beach Bag
- Bug Repellant
- Stain Remover
- Laundry Detergent
- Fiber Absorbent Towel
- Water Bottle
- Ear Plugs
- Eye Mask

ESSENTIALS

- Driver's License
- Money
- Travel Documents
- Credit Cards
- Boarding Pass
- COVID Test Results
- Vaccination Card
- Purse
- Wall

Dr. Melissa Caudle

CRUISE PLANNING GUIDE

Cruise Line: _____ Date of Cruise: _____
Booking #: _____ Transportation to Port: _____
Travel Agent: _____ Phone: (   ) _____
Celebration: _____
Traveling Companions: _____
_____
_____
_____

Day 1 Destination: _____

    Excursion: _____

    What to wear during the day: _____

    What to wear during the evening:_____

Day 2 Destination: _____

    Excursion: _____

    What to wear: _____

    What to wear during the evening:_____

Day 3 Destination: _____

Excursion: _____

    What to wear: _____

Cruising Tips & Hacks from a Professional Cruise Addict

Day 4 Destination: _____

    Excursion: _____

    What to wear: _____

Day 5 Destination: _____

    Excursion: _____

    What to wear: _____

Day 6 Destination: _____

    Excursion: _____

    What to wear: _____

Day 7 Destination: _____

    Excursion: _____

    What to wear: _____

Notes:

_____
_____
_____
_____
_____
_____
_____
_____

Dr. Melissa Caudle

PACKING CHECKLIST

Cruise Line: _____   Date of Cruise: _____
Booking #: _____   Number of Days: _____
Port: _____   Transportation to Port: _____
Destination: _____
Celebration: _____

ESSENTIALS

- Driver's License
- Money
- Travel Documents
- Credit Cards
- Boarding Pass
- COVID Test Results
- Vaccination Card
- Purse
- Wallet

Toiletries

- Toothbrush
- Toothpaste
- Mouthwash
- Shampoo
- Conditioner
- Deodorant
- Razor
- Shaving Cream
- Sunscreen
- Body Lotion
- Aloe Lotion
- Contact Case
- Lip Balm
- Makeup
- Hair Ties
- Bobby Pins
- Makeup Remover
- Styling Gel
- Hairspray

Beach Clothing

- Bathing Suits
- Cover up
- Flip flops
- Water shoes

Cruising Tips & Hacks from a Professional Cruise Addict

Personal Clothing

- Panties
- Bras
- Pajamas
- Socks

Daywear

- 2 Shorts
- 1 Jean
- 2 T-shirts
- 1 Tank Tops

Evening Wear

- 1 Formal Night Attire
- 5 Casual

Outerwear

- Sweater
- Rain Poncho

Shoes

- Tennis Shoes
- Flipflops
- Sandals
- Flats
- Heels

Health and Safety Needs

- First Aid Kit
- OTC Medicines
- Prescription Medicines
- Sunscreen
- Sunglasses
- Allergy Medications
- EpiPen
- Health Insurance Card
- Eyeglasses

Electronics

- Flashlight
- Computer
- iPad
- Phone
- Bluetooth Speaker
- Sun Charger
- Charging Block
- Cords
- Selfie Stick
- Headphones
- Portable Fan
- Camera

Decorations

- Door Magnets
- Plagues
- Whiteboard
- Streamers

Miscellaneous

- Book to Read
- Waterproof Case for Phone
- Beach Bag
- Beach Towel Clips
- Magnetic Hooks
- Duct Tape
- Umbrella
- Backpack
- Lanyard for Cruise Card
- Lanyard for Phone
- Beach Bag
- Bug Repellant
- Stain Remover
- Laundry Detergent
- Fiber Absorbent Towel
- Water Bottle
- Ear Plugs
- Eye Mask

ESSENTIALS

- Driver's License
- Money
- Travel Documents
- Credit Cards
- Boarding Pass
- COVID Test Results
- Vaccination Card
- Purse
- Wallet

Cruising Tips & Hacks from a Professional Cruise Addict

CRUISE PLANNING GUIDE

Cruise Line: _____   Date of Cruise: _____
Booking #: _____   Transportation to Port: _____
Travel Agent: _____   Phone: ( ) _____
Celebration: _____
Traveling Companions: _____
_____
_____
_____

Day 1 Destination: _____

    Excursion: _____

    What to wear during the day: _____

    What to wear during the evening: _____

Day 2 Destination: _____

    Excursion: _____

    What to wear: _____

    What to wear during the evening: _____

Day 3 Destination: _____

Excursion: _____

    What to wear: _____

Day 4 Destination: _____

    Excursion: _____

    What to wear: _____

Day 5 Destination: _____

    Excursion: _____

    What to wear: _____

Day 6 Destination: _____

    Excursion: _____

    What to wear: _____

Day 7 Destination: _____

    Excursion: _____

    What to wear: _____

Notes:
_____
_____
_____
_____
_____
_____
_____

Cruising Tips & Hacks from a Professional Cruise Addict

PACKING CHECKLIST

Cruise Line: _____   Date of Cruise: _____
Booking #: _____   Number of Days: _____
Port: _____   Transportation to Port: _____
Destination: _____
Celebration: _____

ESSENTIALS

- ○ Driver's License
- ○ Money
- ○ Travel Documents
- ○ Credit Cards
- ○ Boarding Pass
- ○ COVID Test Results
- ○ Vaccination Card
- ○ Purse
- ○ Wallet

Toiletries

- ○ Toothbrush
- ○ Toothpaste
- ○ Mouthwash
- ○ Shampoo
- ○ Conditioner
- ○ Deodorant
- ○ Razor
- ○ Shaving Cream
- ○ Sunscreen
- ○ Body Lotion
- ○ Aloe Lotion
- ○ Contact Case
- ○ Lip Balm
- ○ Makeup
- ○ Hair Ties
- ○ Bobby Pins
- ○ Makeup Remover
- ○ Styling Gel
- ○ Hairspray

Beach Clothing

- ○ Bathing Suits
- ○ Cover up
- ○ Flip flops
- ○ Water shoes

Personal Clothing

- Panties
- Bras
- Pajamas
- Socks

Daywear

- 2 Shorts
- 1 Jean
- 2 T-shirts
- 1 Tank Tops

Evening Wear

- 1 Formal Night Attire
- 5 Casual

Outerwear

- Sweater
- Rain Poncho

Shoes

- Tennis Shoes
- Flipflops
- Sandals
- Flats
- Heels

Health and Safety Needs

- First Aid Kit
- OTC Medicines
- Prescription Medicines
- Sunscreen
- Sunglasses
- Allergy Medications
- EpiPen
- Health Insurance Card
- Eyeglasses

Cruising Tips & Hacks from a Professional Cruise Addict

Electronics

- Flashlight
- Computer
- iPad
- Phone
- Bluetooth Speaker
- Sun Charger
- Charging Block
- Cords
- Selfie Stick
- Headphones
- Portable Fan
- Camera

Decorations

- Door Magnets
- Plagues
- Whiteboard
- Streamers

Miscellaneous

- Book to Read
- Waterproof Case for Phone
- Beach Bag
- Beach Towel Clips
- Magnetic Hooks
- Duct Tape
- Umbrella
- Backpack
- Lanyard for Cruise Card
- Lanyard for Phone
- Beach Bag
- Bug Repellant
- Stain Remover
- Laundry Detergent
- Fiber Absorbent Towel
- Water Bottle
- Ear Plugs
- Eye Mask

ESSENTIALS

- Driver's License
- Money
- Travel Documents
- Credit Cards
- Boarding Pass
- COVID Test Results
- Vaccination Card
- Purse
- Walled

131

Dr. Melissa Caudle

CRUISE PLANNING GUIDE

Cruise Line: _____ Date of Cruise: _____
Booking #: _____ Transportation to Port: _____
Travel Agent: _____ Phone: ( ) _____
Celebration: _____
Traveling Companions: _____
_____
_____
_____

Day 1 Destination: _____

    Excursion: _____

    What to wear during the day: _____

    What to wear during the evening: _____

Day 2 Destination: _____

    Excursion: _____

    What to wear: _____

    What to wear during the evening: _____

Day 3 Destination: _____

Excursion: _____

    What to wear: _____

Cruising Tips & Hacks from a Professional Cruise Addict

Day 4 Destination: _____

    Excursion: _____

    What to wear: _____

Day 5 Destination: _____

    Excursion: _____

    What to wear: _____

Day 6 Destination: _____

    Excursion: _____

    What to wear: _____

Day 7 Destination: _____

    Excursion: _____

    What to wear: _____

Notes:
_____
_____
_____
_____
_____
_____
_____
_____

Dr. Melissa Caudle

PACKING CHECKLIST

Cruise Line: _____ Date of Cruise: _____
Booking #: _____ Number of Days: _____
Port: _____ Transportation to Port: _____
Destination: _____
Celebration: _____

ESSENTIALS

- Driver's License
- Money
- Travel Documents
- Credit Cards
- Boarding Pass
- COVID Test Results
- Vaccination Card
- Purse
- Wallet

Toiletries

- Toothbrush
- Toothpaste
- Mouthwash
- Shampoo
- Conditioner
- Deodorant
- Razor
- Shaving Cream
- Sunscreen
- Body Lotion
- Aloe Lotion
- Contact Case
- Lip Balm
- Makeup
- Hair Ties
- Bobby Pins
- Makeup Remover
- Styling Gel
- Hairspray

Beach Clothing

- Bathing Suits
- Cover up
- Flip flops
- Water shoes

Cruising Tips & Hacks from a Professional Cruise Addict

Personal Clothing

- Panties
- Bras
- Pajamas
- Socks

Daywear

- 2 Shorts
- 1 Jean
- 2 T-shirts
- 1 Tank Tops

Evening Wear

- 1 Formal Night Attire
- 5 Casual

Outerwear

- Sweater
- Rain Poncho

Shoes

- Tennis Shoes
- Flipflops
- Sandals
- Flats
- Heels

Health and Safety Needs

- First Aid Kit
- OTC Medicines
- Prescription Medicines
- Sunscreen
- Sunglasses
- Allergy Medications
- EpiPen
- Health Insurance Card
- Eyeglasses

Dr. Melissa Caudle

Electronics

- Flashlight
- Computer
- iPad
- Phone
- Bluetooth Speaker
- Sun Charger
- Charging Block
- Cords
- Selfie Stick
- Headphones
- Portable Fan
- Camera

Decorations

- Door Magnets
- Plagues
- Whiteboard
- Streamers

Miscellaneous

- Book to Read
- Waterproof Case for Phone
- Beach Bag
- Beach Towel Clips
- Magnetic Hooks
- Duct Tape
- Umbrella
- Backpack
- Lanyard for Cruise Card
- Lanyard for Phone
- Beach Bag
- Bug Repellant
- Stain Remover
- Laundry Detergent
- Fiber Absorbent Towel
- Water Bottle
- Ear Plugs
- Eye Mask

ESSENTIALS

- Driver's License
- Money
- Travel Documents
- Credit Cards
- Boarding Pass
- COVID Test Results
- Vaccination Card
- Purse
- Wallet

Cruising Tips & Hacks from a Professional Cruise Addict

CRUISE PLANNING GUIDE

Cruise Line: _____ Date of Cruise: _____
Booking #: _____ Transportation to Port: _____
Travel Agent: _____ Phone: ( ) _____
Celebration: _____
Traveling Companions: _____
_____
_____
_____

Day 1 Destination: _____

    Excursion: _____

    What to wear during the day: _____

    What to wear during the evening: _____

Day 2 Destination: _____

    Excursion: _____

    What to wear: _____

    What to wear during the evening: _____

Day 3 Destination: _____

Excursion: _____

    What to wear: _____

Day 4 Destination: _____

    Excursion: _____

    What to wear: _____

Day 5 Destination: _____

    Excursion: _____

    What to wear: _____

Day 6 Destination: _____

    Excursion: _____

    What to wear: _____

Day 7 Destination: _____

    Excursion: _____

    What to wear: _____

Notes:

_____
_____
_____
_____
_____
_____
_____
_____

Cruising Tips & Hacks from a Professional Cruise Addict

PACKING CHECKLIST

Cruise Line: _____ Date of Cruise: _____
Booking #: _____ Number of Days: _____
Port: _____ Transportation to Port: _____
Destination: _____
Celebration: _____

ESSENTIALS

- Driver's License
- Money
- Travel Documents
- Credit Cards
- Boarding Pass
- COVID Test Results
- Vaccination Card
- Purse
- Wallet

Toiletries

- Toothbrush
- Toothpaste
- Mouthwash
- Shampoo
- Conditioner
- Deodorant
- Razor
- Shaving Cream
- Sunscreen
- Body Lotion
- Aloe Lotion
- Contact Case
- Lip Balm
- Makeup
- Hair Ties
- Bobby Pins
- Makeup Remover
- Styling Gel
- Hairspray

Beach Clothing

- Bathing Suits
- Cover up
- Flip flops
- Water shoes

Personal Clothing

- Panties
- Bras
- Pajamas
- Socks

Daywear

- 2 Shorts
- 1 Jean
- 2 T-shirts
- 1 Tank Tops

Evening Wear

- 1 Formal Night Attire
- 5 Casual

Outerwear

- Sweater
- Rain Poncho

Shoes

- Tennis Shoes
- Flipflops
- Sandals
- Flats
- Heels

Health and Safety Needs

- First Aid Kit
- OTC Medicines
- Prescription Medicines
- Sunscreen
- Sunglasses
- Allergy Medications
- EpiPen
- Health Insurance Card
- Eyeglasses

Cruising Tips & Hacks from a Professional Cruise Addict

Electronics

- Flashlight
- Computer
- iPad
- Phone
- Bluetooth Speaker
- Sun Charger
- Charging Block
- Cords
- Selfie Stick
- Headphones
- Portable Fan
- Camera

Decorations

- Door Magnets
- Plagues
- Whiteboard
- Streamer

Miscellaneous

- Book to Read
- Waterproof Case for Phone
- Beach Bag
- Beach Towel Clips
- Magnetic Hooks
- Duct Tape
- Umbrella
- Backpack
- Lanyard for Cruise Card
- Lanyard for Phone
- Beach Bag
- Bug Repellant
- Stain Remover
- Laundry Detergent
- Fiber Absorbent Towel
- Water Bottle
- Ear Plugs
- Eye Mask

ESSENTIALS

- Driver's License
- Money
- Travel Documents
- Credit Cards
- Boarding Pass
- COVID Test Results
- Vaccination Card
- Purse
- Wallet

Dr. Melissa Caudle

CRUISE PLANNING GUIDE

Cruise Line: _____ Date of Cruise: _____
Booking #: _____ Transportation to Port: _____
Travel Agent: _____ Phone: ( ) _____
Celebration: _____
Traveling Companions: _____
_____
_____
_____

Day 1 Destination: _____

    Excursion: _____

    What to wear during the day: _____

    What to wear during the evening: _____

Day 2 Destination: _____

    Excursion: _____

    What to wear: _____

    What to wear during the evening: _____

Day 3 Destination: _____

Excursion: _____

    What to wear: _____

Cruising Tips & Hacks from a Professional Cruise Addict

Day 4 Destination: _____

    Excursion: _____

    What to wear: _____

Day 5 Destination: _____

    Excursion: _____

    What to wear: _____

Day 6 Destination: _____

    Excursion: _____

    What to wear: _____

Day 7 Destination: _____

    Excursion: _____

    What to wear: _____

Notes:

_____
_____
_____
_____
_____
_____
_____
_____

Dr. Melissa Caudle

PACKING CHECKLIST

Cruise Line: _____ Date of Cruise: _____
Booking #: _____ Number of Days: _____
Port: _____ Transportation to Port: _____
Destination: _____
Celebration: _____

ESSENTIALS

- Driver's License
- Money
- Travel Documents
- Credit Cards
- Boarding Pass
- COVID Test Results
- Vaccination Card
- Purse
- Wallet

Toiletries

- Toothbrush
- Toothpaste
- Mouthwash
- Shampoo
- Conditioner
- Deodorant
- Razor
- Shaving Cream
- Sunscreen
- Body Lotion
- Aloe Lotion
- Contact Case
- Lip Balm
- Makeup
- Hair Ties
- Bobby Pins
- Makeup Remover
- Styling Gel
- Hairspray

Beach Clothing

- Bathing Suits
- Cover up
- Flip flops
- Water shoes

Cruising Tips & Hacks from a Professional Cruise Addict

Personal Clothing

- Panties
- Bras
- Pajamas
- Socks

Daywear

- 2 Shorts
- 1 Jean
- 2 T-shirts
- 1 Tank Tops

Evening Wear

- 1 Formal Night Attire
- 5 Casual

Outerwear

- Sweater
- Rain Poncho

Shoes

- Tennis Shoes
- Flipflops
- Sandals
- Flats
- Heels

Health and Safety Needs

- First Aid Kit
- OTC Medicines
- Prescription Medicines
- Sunscreen
- Sunglasses
- Allergy Medications
- EpiPen
- Health Insurance Card
- Eyeglasses

Electronics

- Flashlight
- Computer
- iPad
- Phone
- Bluetooth Speaker
- Sun Charger
- Charging Block
- Cords
- Selfie Stick
- Headphones
- Portable Fan
- Camera

Decorations

- Door Magnets
- Plagues
- Whiteboard
- Streamers

Miscellaneous

- Book to Read
- Waterproof Case for Phone
- Beach Bag
- Beach Towel Clips
- Magnetic Hooks
- Duct Tape
- Umbrella
- Backpack
- Lanyard for Cruise Card
- Lanyard for Phone
- Beach Bag
- Bug Repellant
- Stain Remover
- Laundry Detergent
- Fiber Absorbent Towel
- Water Bottle
- Ear Plugs
- Eye Mask

ESSENTIALS

- Driver's License
- Money
- Travel Documents
- Credit Cards
- Boarding Pass
- COVID Test Results
- Vaccination Card
- Purse
- Wallet

Cruising Tips & Hacks from a Professional Cruise Addict

CRUISE PLANNING GUIDE

Cruise Line: _____ Date of Cruise: _____
Booking #: _____ Transportation to Port: _____
Travel Agent: _____ Phone: ( ) _____
Celebration: _____
Traveling Companions: _____
_____
_____
_____

Day 1 Destination: _____

    Excursion: _____

    What to wear during the day: _____

    What to wear during the evening: _____

Day 2 Destination: _____

    Excursion: _____

    What to wear: _____

    What to wear during the evening: _____

Day 3 Destination: _____

Excursion: _____

    What to wear: _____

Day 4 Destination: _____

    Excursion: _____

    What to wear: _____

Day 5 Destination: _____

    Excursion: _____

    What to wear: _____

Day 6 Destination: _____

    Excursion: _____

    What to wear: _____

Day 7 Destination: _____

    Excursion: _____

    What to wear: _____

Notes:
_____
_____
_____
_____
_____
_____
_____

Cruising Tips & Hacks from a Professional Cruise Addict

PACKING CHECKLIST

Cruise Line: _____ Date of Cruise: _____
Booking #: _____ Number of Days: _____
Port: _____ Transportation to Port: _____
Destination: _____
Celebration: _____

ESSENTIALS

- Driver's License
- Money
- Travel Documents
- Credit Cards
- Boarding Pass
- COVID Test Results
- Vaccination Card
- Purse
- Wallet

Toiletries

- Toothbrush
- Toothpaste
- Mouthwash
- Shampoo
- Conditioner
- Deodorant
- Razor
- Shaving Cream
- Sunscreen
- Body Lotion
- Aloe Lotion
- Contact Case
- Lip Balm
- Makeup
- Hair Ties
- Bobby Pins
- Makeup Remover
- Styling Gel
- Hairspray

Beach Clothing

- Bathing Suits
- Cover up
- Flip flops
- Water shoes

Dr. Melissa Caudle

Personal Clothing

- Panties
- Bras
- Pajamas
- Socks

Daywear

- 2 Shorts
- 1 Jean
- 2 T-shirts
- 1 Tank Tops

Evening Wear

- 1 Formal Night Attire
- 5 Casual

Outerwear

- Sweater
- Rain Poncho

Shoes

- Tennis Shoes
- Flipflops
- Sandals
- Flats
- Heels

Health and Safety Needs

- First Aid Kit
- OTC Medicines
- Prescription Medicines
- Sunscreen
- Sunglasses
- Allergy Medications
- EpiPen
- Health Insurance Card
- Eyeglasses

Cruising Tips & Hacks from a Professional Cruise Addict

Electronics

- Flashlight
- Computer
- iPad
- Phone

- Bluetooth Speaker
- Sun Charger
- Charging Block

- Cords
- Selfie Stick
- Headphones
- Portable Fan
- Camera

Decorations

- Door Magnets

- Plagues
- Whiteboard

- Streamers

Miscellaneous

- Book to Read
- Waterproof Case for Phone
- Beach Bag
- Beach Towel Clips
- Magnetic Hooks
- Duct Tape

- Umbrella
- Backpack
- Lanyard for Cruise Card
- Lanyard for Phone
- Beach Bag
- Bug Repellant
- Stain Remover

- Laundry Detergent
- Fiber Absorbent Towel
- Water Bottle
- Ear Plugs
- Eye Mask

ESSENTIALS

- Driver's License
- Money
- Travel Documents

- Credit Cards
- Boarding Pass
- COVID Test Results

- Vaccination Card
- Purse
- Wallet

151

Dr. Melissa Caudle

CRUISE PLANNING GUIDE

Cruise Line: _____ **Date of Cruise:** _____
Booking #: _____ **Transportation to Port:** _____
Travel Agent: _____ **Phone:** ( ) _____
Celebration: _____
Traveling Companions: _____
_____
_____
_____

Day 1 Destination: _____

    Excursion: _____

    What to wear during the day: _____

    What to wear during the evening: _____

Day 2 Destination: _____

    Excursion: _____

    What to wear: _____

    What to wear during the evening: _____

Day 3 Destination: _____

Excursion: _____

    What to wear: _____

Cruising Tips & Hacks from a Professional Cruise Addict

Day 4 Destination: _____

    Excursion: _____

    What to wear: _____

Day 5 Destination: _____

    Excursion: _____

    What to wear: _____

Day 6 Destination: _____

    Excursion: _____

    What to wear: _____

Day 7 Destination: _____

    Excursion: _____

    What to wear: _____

Notes:
_____
_____
_____
_____
_____
_____
_____
_____

Dr. Melissa Caudle

PACKING CHECKLIST

Cruise Line: _____ Date of Cruise: _____
Booking #: _____ Number of Days: _____
Port: _____ Transportation to Port: _____
Destination: _____
Celebration: _____

ESSENTIALS

- Driver's License
- Money
- Travel Documents
- Credit Cards
- Boarding Pass
- COVID Test Results
- Vaccination Card
- Purse
- Wallet

Toiletries

- Toothbrush
- Toothpaste
- Mouthwash
- Shampoo
- Conditioner
- Deodorant
- Razor
- Shaving Cream
- Sunscreen
- Body Lotion
- Aloe Lotion
- Contact Case
- Lip Balm
- Makeup
- Hair Ties
- Bobby Pins
- Makeup Remover
- Styling Gel
- Hairspray

Beach Clothing

- Bathing Suits
- Cover up
- Flip flops
- Water shoes

Cruising Tips & Hacks from a Professional Cruise Addict

Personal Clothing

- Panties
- Bras
- Pajamas
- Socks

Daywear

- 2 Shorts
- 1 Jean
- 2 T-shirts
- 1 Tank Tops

Evening Wear

- 1 Formal Night Attire
- 5 Casual

Outerwear

- Sweater
- Rain Poncho

Shoes

- Tennis Shoes
- Flipflops
- Sandals
- Flats
- Heels

Health and Safety Needs

- First Aid Kit
- OTC Medicines
- Prescription Medicines
- Sunscreen
- Sunglasses
- Allergy Medications
- EpiPen
- Health Insurance Card
- Eyeglasses

Dr. Melissa Caudle

Electronics

- Flashlight
- Computer
- iPad
- Phone
- Bluetooth Speaker
- Sun Charger
- Charging Block
- Cords
- Selfie Stick
- Headphones
- Portable Fan
- Camera

Decorations

- Door Magnets
- Plagues
- Whiteboard
- Streamers

Miscellaneous

- Book to Read
- Waterproof Case for Phone
- Beach Bag
- Beach Towel Clips
- Magnetic Hooks
- Duct Tape
- Umbrella
- Backpack
- Lanyard for Cruise Card
- Lanyard for Phone
- Beach Bag
- Bug Repellant
- Stain Remover
- Laundry Detergent
- Fiber Absorbent Towel
- Water Bottle
- Ear Plugs
- Eye Mask

ESSENTIALS

- Driver's License
- Money
- Travel Documents
- Credit Cards
- Boarding Pass
- COVID Test Results
- Vaccination Card
- Purse
- Wallet

Cruising Tips & Hacks from a Professional Cruise Addict

CRUISE PLANNING GUIDE

Cruise Line: _____ **Date of Cruise:** _____
Booking #: _____ **Transportation to Port:** _____
Travel Agent: _____ **Phone: (   )** _____
Celebration: _____
Traveling Companions: _____
_____
_____
_____

Day 1 Destination: _____

   Excursion: _____

   What to wear during the day: _____

   What to wear during the evening: _____

Day 2 Destination: _____

   Excursion: _____

   What to wear: _____

   What to wear during the evening: _____

Day 3 Destination: _____

Excursion: _____

   What to wear: _____

Day 4 Destination: _____

    Excursion: _____

    What to wear: _____

Day 5 Destination: _____

    Excursion: _____

    What to wear: _____

Day 6 Destination: _____

    Excursion: _____

    What to wear: _____

Day 7 Destination: _____

    Excursion: _____

    What to wear: _____

Notes:

_____
_____
_____
_____
_____
_____
_____

Cruising Tips & Hacks from a Professional Cruise Addict

PACKING CHECKLIST

Cruise Line: _____ Date of Cruise: _____
Booking #: _____ Number of Days: _____
Port: _____ Transportation to Port: _____
Destination: _____
Celebration: _____

ESSENTIALS

- ☐ Driver's License
- ☐ Money
- ☐ Travel Documents
- ☐ Credit Cards
- ☐ Boarding Pass
- ☐ COVID Test Results
- ☐ Vaccination Card
- ☐ Purse
- ☐ Wallet

Toiletries

- ☐ Toothbrush
- ☐ Toothpaste
- ☐ Mouthwash
- ☐ Shampoo
- ☐ Conditioner
- ☐ Deodorant
- ☐ Razor
- ☐ Shaving Cream
- ☐ Sunscreen
- ☐ Body Lotion
- ☐ Aloe Lotion
- ☐ Contact Case
- ☐ Lip Balm
- ☐ Makeup
- ☐ Hair Ties
- ☐ Bobby Pins
- ☐ Makeup Remover
- ☐ Styling Gel
- ☐ Hairspray

Beach Clothing

- ☐ Bathing Suits
- ☐ Cover up
- ☐ Flip flops
- ☐ Water shoes

Dr. Melissa Caudle

Personal Clothing

- Panties
- Bras
- Pajamas
- Socks

Daywear

- 2 Shorts
- 1 Jean
- 2 T-shirts
- 1 Tank Tops

Evening Wear

- 1 Formal Night Attire
- 5 Casual

Outerwear

- Sweater
- Rain Poncho

Shoes

- Tennis Shoes
- Flipflops
- Sandals
- Flats
- Heels

Health and Safety Needs

- First Aid Kit
- OTC Medicines
- Prescription Medicines
- Sunscreen
- Sunglasses
- Allergy Medications
- EpiPen
- Health Insurance Card
- Eyeglasses

Cruising Tips & Hacks from a Professional Cruise Addict

Electronics

- Flashlight
- Computer
- iPad
- Phone
- Bluetooth Speaker
- Sun Charger
- Charging Block
- Cords
- Selfie Stick
- Headphones
- Portable Fan
- Camera

Decorations

- Door Magnets
- Plagues
- Whiteboard
- Streamers

Miscellaneous

- Book to Read
- Waterproof Case for Phone
- Beach Bag
- Beach Towel Clips
- Magnetic Hooks
- Duct Tape
- Umbrella
- Backpack
- Lanyard for Cruise Card
- Lanyard for Phone
- Beach Bag
- Bug Repellant
- Stain Remover
- Laundry Detergent
- Fiber Absorbent Towel
- Water Bottle
- Ear Plugs
- Eye Mask

ESSENTIALS

- Driver's License
- Money
- Travel Documents
- Credit Cards
- Boarding Pass
- COVID Test Results
- Vaccination Card
- Purse
- Wallet

Dr. Melissa Caudle

CRUISE PLANNING GUIDE

Cruise Line: _____ Date of Cruise: _____
Booking #: _____ Transportation to Port: _____
Travel Agent: _____ Phone: (   ) _____
Celebration: _____
Traveling Companions: _____
_____
_____
_____

Day 1 Destination: _____

    Excursion: _____

    What to wear during the day: _____

    What to wear during the evening: _____

Day 2 Destination: _____

    Excursion: _____

    What to wear: _____

    What to wear during the evening: _____

Day 3 Destination: _____

Excursion: _____

    What to wear: _____

Cruising Tips & Hacks from a Professional Cruise Addict

Day 4 Destination: _____

    Excursion: _____

    What to wear: _____

Day 5 Destination: _____

    Excursion: _____

    What to wear: _____

Day 6 Destination: _____

    Excursion: _____

    What to wear: _____

Day 7 Destination: _____

    Excursion: _____

    What to wear: _____

Notes:
_____
_____
_____
_____
_____
_____
_____
_____

Dr. Melissa Caudle

PACKING CHECKLIST

Cruise Line: _____ Date of Cruise: _____
Booking #: _____ Number of Days: _____
Port: _____ Transportation to Port: _____
Destination: _____
Celebration: _____

ESSENTIALS

- Driver's License
- Money
- Travel Documents
- Credit Cards
- Boarding Pass
- COVID Test Results
- Vaccination Card
- Purse
- Wallet

Toiletries

- Toothbrush
- Toothpaste
- Mouthwash
- Shampoo
- Conditioner
- Deodorant
- Razor
- Shaving Cream
- Sunscreen
- Body Lotion
- Aloe Lotion
- Contact Case
- Lip Balm
- Makeup
- Hair Ties
- Bobby Pins
- Makeup Remover
- Styling Gel
- Hairspray

Beach Clothing

- Bathing Suits
- Cover up
- Flip flops
- Water shoes

Cruising Tips & Hacks from a Professional Cruise Addict

Personal Clothing

- Panties
- Bras
- Pajamas
- Socks

Daywear

- 2 Shorts
- 1 Jean
- 2 T-shirts
- 1 Tank Tops

Evening Wear

- 1 Formal Night Attire
- 5 Casual

Outerwear

- Sweater
- Rain Poncho

Shoes

- Tennis Shoes
- Flipflops
- Sandals
- Flats
- Heels

Health and Safety Needs

- First Aid Kit
- OTC Medicines
- Prescription Medicines
- Sunscreen
- Sunglasses
- Allergy Medications
- EpiPen
- Health Insurance Card
- Eyeglasses

Dr. Melissa Caudle

Electronics

- Flashlight
- Computer
- iPad
- Phone
- Bluetooth Speaker
- Sun Charger
- Charging Block
- Cords
- Selfie Stick
- Headphones
- Portable Fan
- Camera

Decorations

- Door Magnets
- Plagues
- Whiteboard
- Streamers

Miscellaneous

- Book to Read
- Waterproof Case for Phone
- Beach Bag
- Beach Towel Clips
- Magnetic Hooks
- Duct Tape
- Umbrella
- Backpack
- Lanyard for Cruise Card
- Lanyard for Phone
- Beach Bag
- Bug Repellant
- Stain Remover
- Laundry Detergent
- Fiber Absorbent Towel
- Water Bottle
- Ear Plugs
- Eye Mask

ESSENTIALS

- Driver's License
- Money
- Travel Documents
- Credit Cards
- Boarding Pass
- COVID Test Results
- Vaccination Card
- Purse
- wallet

Cruising Tips & Hacks from a Professional Cruise Addict

CRUISE PLANNING GUIDE

Cruise Line: _____ Date of Cruise: _____
Booking #: _____ Transportation to Port: _____
Travel Agent: _____ Phone: ( ) _____
Celebration: _____
Traveling Companions: _____
_____
_____
_____

Day 1 Destination: _____

    Excursion: _____

    What to wear during the day: _____

    What to wear during the evening: _____

Day 2 Destination: _____

    Excursion: _____

    What to wear: _____

    What to wear during the evening: _____

Day 3 Destination: _____

Excursion: _____

    What to wear: _____

Day 4 Destination: _____

    Excursion: _____

    What to wear: _____

Day 5 Destination: _____

    Excursion: _____

    What to wear: _____

Day 6 Destination: _____

    Excursion: _____

    What to wear: _____

Day 7 Destination: _____

    Excursion: _____

    What to wear: _____

Notes:
_____
_____
_____
_____
_____
_____
_____
_____

Cruising Tips & Hacks from a Professional Cruise Addict

PACKING CHECKLIST

Cruise Line: _____ **Date of Cruise:** _____
Booking #: _____ **Number of Days:** _____
Port: _____ **Transportation to Port:** _____
Destination: _____
Celebration: _____

ESSENTIALS

- Driver's License
- Money
- Travel Documents
- Credit Cards
- Boarding Pass
- COVID Test Results
- Vaccination Card
- Purse
- Wallet

Toiletries

- Toothbrush
- Toothpaste
- Mouthwash
- Shampoo
- Conditioner
- Deodorant
- Razor
- Shaving Cream
- Sunscreen
- Body Lotion
- Aloe Lotion
- Contact Case
- Lip Balm
- Makeup
- Hair Ties
- Bobby Pins
- Makeup Remover
- Styling Gel
- Hairspray

Beach Clothing

- Bathing Suits
- Cover up
- Flip flops
- Water shoes

Personal Clothing

- Panties
- Bras
- Pajamas
- Socks

Daywear

- 2 Shorts
- 1 Jean
- 2 T-shirts
- 1 Tank Tops

Evening Wear

- 1 Formal Night Attire
- 5 Casual

Outerwear

- Sweater
- Rain Poncho

Shoes

- Tennis Shoes
- Flipflops
- Sandals
- Flats
- Heels

Health and Safety Needs

- First Aid Kit
- OTC Medicines
- Prescription Medicines
- Sunscreen
- Sunglasses
- Allergy Medications
- EpiPen
- Health Insurance Card
- Eyeglasses

Cruising Tips & Hacks from a Professional Cruise Addict

Electronics

- Flashlight
- Computer
- iPad
- Phone
- Bluetooth Speaker
- Sun Charger
- Charging Block
- Cords
- Se fie Stick
- Headphones
- Portable Fan
- Camera

Decorations

- Door Magnets
- Plagues
- Whiteboard
- Streamers

Miscellaneous

- Book to Read
- Waterproof Case for Phone
- Beach Bag
- Beach Towel Clips
- Magnetic Hooks
- Duct Tape
- Umbrella
- Backpack
- Lanyard for Cruise Card
- Lanyard for Phone
- Beach Bag
- Bug Repellant
- Stain Remover
- Laundry Detergent
- Fiber Absorbent Towel
- Water Bottle
- Ear Plugs
- Eye Mask

ESSENTIALS

- Driver's License
- Money
- Travel Documents
- Credit Cards
- Boarding Pass
- COVID Test Results
- Vaccination Card
- Purse
- Wallet

Dr. Melissa Caudle

CRUISE PLANNING GUIDE

Cruise Line: _____ Date of Cruise: _____
Booking #: _____ Transportation to Port: _____
Travel Agent: _____ Phone: ( ) _____
Celebration: _____
Traveling Companions: _____
_____
_____
_____

Day 1 Destination: _____

    Excursion: _____

    What to wear during the day: _____

    What to wear during the evening: _____

Day 2 Destination: _____

    Excursion: _____

    What to wear: _____

    What to wear during the evening: _____

Day 3 Destination: _____

Excursion: _____

    What to wear: _____

Cruising Tips & Hacks from a Professional Cruise Addict

Day 4 Destination: _____

    Excursion: _____

    What to wear: _____

Day 5 Destination: _____

    Excursion: _____

    What to wear: _____

Day 6 Destination: _____

    Excursion: _____

    What to wear: _____

Day 7 Destination: _____

    Excursion: _____

    What to wear: _____

Notes:
_____
_____
_____
_____
_____
_____
_____

Dr. Melissa Caudle

PACKING CHECKLIST

Cruise Line: _____ Date of Cruise: _____
Booking #: _____ Number of Days: _____
Port: _____ Transportation to Port: _____
Destination: _____
Celebration: _____

ESSENTIALS

- Driver's License
- Money
- Travel Documents
- Credit Cards
- Boarding Pass
- COVID Test Results
- Vaccination Card
- Purse
- Wallet

Toiletries

- Toothbrush
- Toothpaste
- Mouthwash
- Shampoo
- Conditioner
- Deodorant
- Razor
- Shaving Cream
- Sunscreen
- Body Lotion
- Aloe Lotion
- Contact Case
- Lip Balm
- Makeup
- Hair Ties
- Bobby Pins
- Makeup Remover
- Styling Gel
- Hairspray

Beach Clothing

- Bathing Suits
- Cover up
- Flip flops
- Water shoes

Cruising Tips & Hacks from a Professional Cruise Addict

Personal Clothing

- Panties
- Bras
- Pajamas
- Socks

Daywear

- 2 Shorts
- 1 Jean
- 2 T-shirts
- 1 Tank Tops

Evening Wear

- 1 Formal Night Attire
- 5 Casual

Outerwear

- Sweater
- Rain Poncho

Shoes

- Tennis Shoes
- Flipflops
- Sandals
- Flats
- Heels

Health and Safety Needs

- First Aid Kit
- OTC Medicines
- Prescription Medicines
- Sunscreen
- Sunglasses
- Allergy Medications
- EpiPen
- Health Insurance Card
- Eyeglasses

Dr. Melissa Caudle

Electronics

- Flashlight
- Computer
- iPad
- Phone
- Bluetooth Speaker
- Sun Charger
- Charging Block
- Cords
- Selfie Stick
- Headphones
- Portable Fan
- Camera

Decorations

- Door Magnets
- Plagues
- Whiteboard
- Streamers

Miscellaneous

- Book to Read
- Waterproof Case for Phone
- Beach Bag
- Beach Towel Clips
- Magnetic Hooks
- Duct Tape
- Umbrella
- Backpack
- Lanyard for Cruise Card
- Lanyard for Phone
- Beach Bag
- Bug Repellant
- Stain Remover
- Laundry Detergent
- Fiber Absorbent Towel
- Water Bottle
- Ear Plugs
- Eye Mask

ESSENTIALS

- Driver's License
- Money
- Travel Documents
- Credit Cards
- Boarding Pass
- COVID Test Results
- Vaccination Card
- Purse
- Wallet

Cruising Tips & Hacks from a Professional Cruise Addict

CRUISE PLANNING GUIDE

Cruise Line: _____ Date of Cruise: _____
Booking #: _____ Transportation to Port: _____
Travel Agent: _____ Phone: (   ) _____
Celebration: _____
Traveling Companions: _____
_____
_____
_____

Day 1 Destination: _____

    Excursion: _____

    What to wear during the day: _____

    What to wear during the evening: _____

Day 2 Destination: _____

    Excursion: _____

    What to wear: _____

    What to wear during the evening: _____

Day 3 Destination: _____

Excursion: _____

    What to wear: _____

Day 4 Destination: _____

    Excursion: _____

    What to wear: _____

Day 5 Destination: _____

    Excursion: _____

    What to wear: _____

Day 6 Destination: _____

    Excursion: _____

    What to wear: _____

Day 7 Destination: _____

    Excursion: _____

    What to wear: _____

Notes:
_____
_____
_____
_____
_____
_____
_____

Cruising Tips & Hacks from a Professional Cruise Addict

PACKING CHECKLIST

Cruise Line: _____ Date of Cruise: _____
Booking #: _____ Number of Days: _____
Port: _____ Transportation to Port: _____
Destination: _____
Celebration: _____

ESSENTIALS

- Driver's License
- Money
- Travel Documents
- Credit Cards
- Boarding Pass
- COVID Test Results
- Vaccination Card
- Purse
- Wallet

Toiletries

- Toothbrush
- Toothpaste
- Mouthwash
- Shampoo
- Conditioner
- Deodorant
- Razor
- Shaving Cream
- Sunscreen
- Body Lotion
- Aloe Lotion
- Contact Case
- Lip Balm
- Makeup
- Hair Ties
- Bobby Pins
- Makeup Remover
- Styling Gel
- Hairspray

Beach Clothing

- Bathing Suits
- Cover up
- Flip flops
- Water shoes

Dr. Melissa Caudle

Personal Clothing

- Panties
- Bras
- Pajamas
- Socks

Daywear

- 2 Shorts
- 1 Jean
- 2 T-shirts
- 1 Tank Tops

Evening Wear

- 1 Formal Night Attire
- 5 Casual

Outerwear

- Sweater
- Rain Poncho

Shoes

- Tennis Shoes
- Flipflops
- Sandals
- Flats
- Heels

Health and Safety Needs

- First Aid Kit
- OTC Medicines
- Prescription Medicines
- Sunscreen
- Sunglasses
- Allergy Medications
- EpiPen
- Health Insurance Card
- Eyeglasses

Cruising Tips & Hacks from a Professional Cruise Addict

Electronics

- Flashlight
- Computer
- iPad
- Phone
- Bluetooth Speaker
- Sun Charger
- Charging Block
- Cords
- Selfie Stick
- Headphones
- Portable Fan
- Camera

Decorations

- Door Magnets
- Plagues
- Whiteboard
- Streamers

Miscellaneous

- Book to Read
- Waterproof Case for Phone
- Beach Bag
- Beach Towel Clips
- Magnetic Hooks
- Duct Tape
- Umbrella
- Backpack
- Lanyard for Cruise Card
- Lanyard for Phone
- Beach Bag
- Bug Repellant
- Stain Remover
- Laundry Detergent
- Fiber Absorbent Towel
- Water Bottle
- Ear Plugs
- Eye Mask

ESSENTIALS

- Driver's License
- Money
- Travel Documents
- Credit Cards
- Boarding Pass
- COVID Test Results
- Vaccination Card
- Purse
- Wallet

181

Dr. Melissa Caudle

CRUISE PLANNING GUIDE

Cruise Line: _____ Date of Cruise: _____
Booking #: _____ Transportation to Port: _____
Travel Agent: _____ Phone: (   ) _____
Celebration: _____
Traveling Companions: _____
_____
_____
_____

Day 1 Destination: _____

    Excursion: _____

    What to wear during the day: _____

    What to wear during the evening: _____

Day 2 Destination: _____

    Excursion: _____

    What to wear: _____

    What to wear during the evening: _____

Day 3 Destination: _____

Excursion: _____

    What to wear: _____

Cruising Tips & Hacks from a Professional Cruise Addict

Day 4 Destination: _____

    Excursion: _____

    What to wear: _____

Day 5 Destination: _____

    Excursion: _____

    What to wear: _____

Day 6 Destination: _____

    Excursion: _____

    What to wear: _____

Day 7 Destination: _____

    Excursion: _____

    What to wear: _____

Notes:
_____
_____
_____
_____
_____
_____
_____
_____

Dr. Melissa Caudle

PACKING CHECKLIST

Cruise Line: _____   Date of Cruise: _____
Booking #: _____   Number of Days: _____
Port: _____   Transportation to Port: _____
Destination: _____
Celebration: _____

ESSENTIALS

- Driver's License
- Money
- Travel Documents
- Credit Cards
- Boarding Pass
- COVID Test Results
- Vaccination Card
- Purse
- Wallet

Toiletries

- Toothbrush
- Toothpaste
- Mouthwash
- Shampoo
- Conditioner
- Deodorant
- Razor
- Shaving Cream
- Sunscreen
- Body Lotion
- Aloe Lotion
- Contact Case
- Lip Balm
- Makeup
- Hair Ties
- Bobby Pins
- Makeup Remover
- Styling Gel
- Hairspray

Beach Clothing

- Bathing Suits
- Cover up
- Flip flops
- Water shoes

Cruising Tips & Hacks from a Professional Cruise Addict

Personal Clothing

- Panties
- Bras
- Pajamas
- Socks

Daywear

- 2 Shorts
- 1 Jean
- 2 T-shirts
- 1 Tank Tops

Evening Wear

- 1 Formal Night Attire
- 5 Casual

Outerwear

- Sweater
- Rain Poncho

Shoes

- Tennis Shoes
- Flipflops
- Sandals
- Flats
- Heels

Health and Safety Needs

- First Aid Kit
- OTC Medicines
- Prescription Medicines
- Sunscreen
- Sunglasses
- Allergy Medications
- EpiPen
- Health Insurance Card
- Eyeglasses

Dr. Melissa Caudle

Electronics

- Flashlight
- Computer
- iPad
- Phone
- Bluetooth Speaker
- Sun Charger
- Charging Block
- Cords
- Selfie Stick
- Headphones
- Portable Fan
- Camera

Decorations

- Door Magnets
- Plagues
- Whiteboard
- Streamers

Miscellaneous

- Book to Read
- Waterproof Case for Phone
- Beach Bag
- Beach Towel Clips
- Magnetic Hooks
- Duct Tape
- Umbrella
- Backpack
- Lanyard for Cruise Card
- Lanyard for Phone
- Beach Bag
- Bug Repellant
- Stain Remover
- Laundry Detergent
- Fiber Absorbent Towel
- Water Bottle
- Ear Plugs
- Eye Mask

ESSENTIALS

- Driver's License
- Money
- Travel Documents
- Credit Cards
- Boarding Pass
- COVID Test Results
- Vaccination Card
- Purse
- Wallet

Cruising Tips & Hacks from a Professional Cruise Addict

CRUISE PLANNING GUIDE

Cruise Line: _____ Date of Cruise: _____
Booking #: _____ Transportation to Port: _____
Travel Agent: _____ Phone: ( ) _____
Celebration: _____
Traveling Companions: _____
_____
_____
_____

Day 1 Destination: _____

    Excursion: _____

    What to wear during the day: _____

    What to wear during the evening: _____

Day 2 Destination: _____

    Excursion: _____

    What to wear: _____

    What to wear during the evening: _____

Day 3 Destination: _____

Excursion: _____

    What to wear: _____

Day 4 Destination: _____

    Excursion: _____

    What to wear: _____

Day 5 Destination: _____

    Excursion: _____

    What to wear: _____

Day 6 Destination: _____

    Excursion: _____

    What to wear: _____

Day 7 Destination: _____

    Excursion: _____

    What to wear: _____

Notes:

_____
_____
_____
_____
_____
_____
_____

Cruising Tips & Hacks from a Professional Cruise Addict

PACKING CHECKLIST

Cruise Line: _____   Date of Cruise: _____
Booking #: _____   Number of Days: _____
Port: _____   Transportation to Port: _____
Destination: _____
Celebration: _____

ESSENTIALS

- ☐ Driver's License
- ☐ Money
- ☐ Travel Documents
- ☐ Credit Cards
- ☐ Boarding Pass
- ☐ COVID Test Results
- ☐ Vaccination Card
- ☐ Purse
- ☐ Wallet

Toiletries

- ☐ Toothbrush
- ☐ Toothpaste
- ☐ Mouthwash
- ☐ Shampoo
- ☐ Conditioner
- ☐ Deodorant
- ☐ Razor
- ☐ Shaving Cream
- ☐ Sunscreen
- ☐ Body Lotion
- ☐ Aloe Lotion
- ☐ Contact Case
- ☐ Lip Balm
- ☐ Makeup
- ☐ Hair Ties
- ☐ Bobby Pins
- ☐ Makeup Remover
- ☐ Styling Gel
- ☐ Hairspray

Beach Clothing

- ☐ Bathing Suits
- ☐ Cover up
- ☐ Flip flops
- ☐ Water shoes

Dr. Melissa Caudle

Personal Clothing

- Panties
- Bras
- Pajamas
- Socks

Daywear

- 2 Shorts
- 1 Jean
- 2 T-shirts
- 1 Tank Tops

Evening Wear

- 1 Formal Night Attire
- 5 Casual

Outerwear

- Sweater
- Rain Poncho

Shoes

- Tennis Shoes
- Flipflops
- Sandals
- Flats
- Heels

Health and Safety Needs

- First Aid Kit
- OTC Medicines
- Prescription Medicines
- Sunscreen
- Sunglasses
- Allergy Medications
- EpiPen
- Health Insurance Card
- Eyeglasses

Cruising Tips & Hacks from a Professional Cruise Addict

Electronics

- Flashlight
- Computer
- iPad
- Phone
- Bluetooth Speaker
- Sun Charger
- Charging Block
- Cords
- Selfie Stick
- Headphones
- Portable Fan
- Camera

Decorations

- Door Magnets
- Plagues
- Whiteboard
- Streamers

Miscellaneous

- Book to Read
- Waterproof Case for Phone
- Beach Bag
- Beach Towel Clips
- Magnetic Hooks
- Duct Tape
- Umbrella
- Backpack
- Lanyard for Cruise Card
- Lanyard for Phone
- Beach Bag
- Bug Repellant
- Stain Remover
- Laundry Detergent
- Fiber Absorbent Towel
- Water Bottle
- Ear Plugs
- Eye Mask

ESSENTIALS

- Driver's License
- Money
- Travel Documents
- Credit Cards
- Boarding Pass
- COVID Test Results
- Vaccination Card
- Purse
- Wallet

Dr. Melissa Caudle

CRUISE PLANNING GUIDE

Cruise Line: _____ Date of Cruise: _____
Booking #: _____ Transportation to Port: _____
Travel Agent: _____ Phone: (   ) _____
Celebration: _____
Traveling Companions: _____
_____
_____
_____

Day 1 Destination: _____

    Excursion: _____

    What to wear during the day: _____

    What to wear during the evening:_____

Day 2 Destination: _____

    Excursion: _____

    What to wear: _____

    What to wear during the evening:_____

Day 3 Destination: _____

Excursion: _____

    What to wear: _____

Cruising Tips & Hacks from a Professional Cruise Addict

Day 4 Destination: _____

    Excursion: _____

    What to wear: _____

Day 5 Destination: _____

    Excursion: _____

    What to wear: _____

Day 6 Destination: _____

    Excursion: _____

    What to wear: _____

Day 7 Destination: _____

    Excursion: _____

    What to wear: _____

Notes:

_____
_____
_____
_____
_____
_____
_____
_____

Dr. Melissa Caudle

PACKING CHECKLIST

Cruise Line: _____ Date of Cruise: _____
Booking #: _____ Number of Days: _____
Port: _____ Transportation to Port: _____
Destination: _____
Celebration: _____

ESSENTIALS

- Driver's License
- Money
- Travel Documents
- Credit Cards
- Boarding Pass
- COVID Test Results
- Vaccination Card
- Purse
- Wallet

Toiletries

- Toothbrush
- Toothpaste
- Mouthwash
- Shampoo
- Conditioner
- Deodorant
- Razor
- Shaving Cream
- Sunscreen
- Body Lotion
- Aloe Lotion
- Contact Case
- Lip Balm
- Makeup
- Hair Ties
- Bobby Pins
- Makeup Remover
- Styling Gel
- Hairspray

Beach Clothing

- Bathing Suits
- Cover up
- Flip flops
- Water shoes

Cruising Tips & Hacks from a Professional Cruise Addict

Personal Clothing

- Panties
- Bras
- Pajamas
- Socks

Daywear

- 2 Shorts
- 1 Jean
- 2 T-shirts
- 1 Tank Tops

Evening Wear

- 1 Formal Night Attire
- 5 Casual

Outerwear

- Sweater
- Rain Poncho

Shoes

- Tennis Shoes
- Flipflops
- Sandals
- Flats
- Heels

Health and Safety Needs

- First Aid Kit
- OTC Medicines
- Prescription Medicines
- Sunscreen
- Sunglasses
- Allergy Medications
- EpiPen
- Health Insurance Card
- Eyeglasses

Dr. Melissa Caudle

Electronics

- Flashlight
- Computer
- iPad
- Phone
- Bluetooth Speaker
- Sun Charger
- Charging Block
- Cords
- Selfie Stick
- Headphones
- Portable Fan
- Camera

Decorations

- Door Magnets
- Plagues
- Whiteboard
- Streamers

Miscellaneous

- Book to Read
- Waterproof Case for Phone
- Beach Bag
- Beach Towel Clips
- Magnetic Hooks
- Duct Tape
- Umbrella
- Backpack
- Lanyard for Cruise Card
- Lanyard for Phone
- Beach Bag
- Bug Repellant
- Stain Remover
- Laundry Detergent
- Fiber Absorbent Towel
- Water Bottle
- Ear Plugs
- Eye Mask

ESSENTIALS

- Driver's License
- Money
- Travel Documents
- Credit Cards
- Boarding Pass
- COVID Test Results
- Vaccination Card
- Purse
- Wallet

Cruising Tips & Hacks from a Professional Cruise Addict

CRUISE PLANNING GUIDE

Cruise Line: _____ Date of Cruise: _____
Booking #: _____ Transportation to Port: _____
Travel Agent: _____ Phone: (   ) _____
Celebration: _____
Traveling Companions: _____
_____
_____
_____

Day 1 Destination: _____

    Excursion: _____

    What to wear during the day: _____

    What to wear during the evening: _____

Day 2 Destination: _____

    Excursion: _____

    What to wear: _____

    What to wear during the evening: _____

Day 3 Destination: _____

Excursion: _____

    What to wear: _____

Day 4 Destination: _____

    Excursion: _____

    What to wear: _____

Day 5 Destination: _____

    Excursion: _____

    What to wear: _____

Day 6 Destination: _____

    Excursion: _____

    What to wear: _____

Day 7 Destination: _____

    Excursion: _____

    What to wear: _____

Notes:

_____
_____
_____
_____
_____
_____
_____

Cruising Tips & Hacks from a Professional Cruise Addict

PACKING CHECKLIST

Cruise Line: _____ **Date of Cruise:** _____
Booking #: _____ **Number of Days:** _____
Port: _____ **Transportation to Port:** _____
Destination: _____
Celebration: _____

ESSENTIALS

- ○ Driver's License
- ○ Money
- ○ Travel Documents
- ○ Credit Cards
- ○ Boarding Pass
- ○ COVID Test Results
- ○ Vaccination Card
- ○ Purse
- ○ Wallet

Toiletries

- ○ Toothbrush
- ○ Toothpaste
- ○ Mouthwash
- ○ Shampoo
- ○ Conditioner
- ○ Deodorant
- ○ Razor
- ○ Shaving Cream
- ○ Sunscreen
- ○ Body Lotion
- ○ Aloe Lotion
- ○ Contact Case
- ○ Lip Balm
- ○ Makeup
- ○ Hair Ties
- ○ Bobby Pins
- ○ Makeup Remover
- ○ Styling Gel
- ○ Hairspray

Beach Clothing

- ○ Bathing Suits
- ○ Cover up
- ○ Flip flops
- ○ Water shoes

Dr. Melissa Caudle

Personal Clothing

- Panties
- Bras
- Pajamas
- Socks

Daywear

- 2 Shorts
- 1 Jean
- 2 T-shirts
- 1 Tank Tops

Evening Wear

- 1 Formal Night Attire
- 5 Casual

Outerwear

- Sweater
- Rain Poncho

Shoes

- Tennis Shoes
- Flipflops
- Sandals
- Flats
- Heels

Health and Safety Needs

- First Aid Kit
- OTC Medicines
- Prescription Medicines
- Sunscreen
- Sunglasses
- Allergy Medications
- EpiPen
- Health Insurance Card
- Eyeglasses

Cruising Tips & Hacks from a Professional Cruise Addict

Electronics

- Flashlight
- Computer
- iPad
- Phone
- Bluetooth Speaker
- Sun Charger
- Charging Block
- Cords
- Selfie Stick
- Headphones
- Portable Fan
- Camera

Decorations

- Door Magnets
- Plagues
- Whiteboard
- Streamers

Miscellaneous

- Book to Read
- Waterproof Case for Phone
- Beach Bag
- Beach Towel Clips
- Magnetic Hooks
- Duct Tape
- Umbrella
- Backpack
- Lanyard for Cruise Card
- Lanyard for Phone
- Beach Bag
- Bug Repellant
- Stain Remover
- Laundry Detergent
- Fiber Absorbent Towel
- Water Bottle
- Ear Plugs
- Eye Mask

ESSENTIALS

- Driver's License
- Money
- Travel Documents
- Credit Cards
- Boarding Pass
- COVID Test Results
- Vaccination Card
- Purse
- Wallet

Dr. Melissa Caudle

CRUISE PLANNING GUIDE

Cruise Line: _____ Date of Cruise: _____
Booking #: _____ Transportation to Port: _____
Travel Agent: _____ Phone: ( ) _____
Celebration: _____
Traveling Companions: _____
_____
_____
_____

Day 1 Destination: _____

    Excursion: _____

    What to wear during the day: _____

    What to wear during the evening: _____

Day 2 Destination: _____

    Excursion: _____

    What to wear: _____

    What to wear during the evening: _____

Day 3 Destination: _____

Excursion: _____

    What to wear: _____

Cruising Tips & Hacks from a Professional Cruise Addict

Day 4 Destination: _____

    Excursion: _____

    What to wear: _____

Day 5 Destination: _____

    Excursion: _____

    What to wear: _____

Day 6 Destination: _____

    Excursion: _____

    What to wear: _____

Day 7 Destination: _____

    Excursion: _____

    What to wear: _____

Notes:

_____
_____
_____
_____
_____
_____
_____

Dr. Melissa Caudle

PACKING CHECKLIST

Cruise Line: _____ Date of Cruise: _____
Booking #: _____ Number of Days: _____
Port: _____ Transportation to Port: _____
Destination: _____
Celebration: _____

ESSENTIALS

- Driver's License
- Money
- Travel Documents
- Credit Cards
- Boarding Pass
- COVID Test Results
- Vaccination Card
- Purse
- Wallet

Toiletries

- Toothbrush
- Toothpaste
- Mouthwash
- Shampoo
- Conditioner
- Deodorant
- Razor
- Shaving Cream
- Sunscreen
- Body Lotion
- Aloe Lotion
- Contact Case
- Lip Balm
- Makeup
- Hair Ties
- Bobby Pins
- Makeup Remover
- Styling Gel
- Hairspray

Beach Clothing

- Bathing Suits
- Cover up
- Flip flops
- Water shoes

Cruising Tips & Hacks from a Professional Cruise Addict

Personal Clothing

- Panties
- Bras
- Pajamas
- Socks

Daywear

- 2 Shorts
- 1 Jean
- 2 T-shirts
- 1 Tank Tops

Evening Wear

- 1 Formal Night Attire
- 5 Casual

Outerwear

- Sweater
- Rain Poncho

Shoes

- Tennis Shoes
- Flipflops
- Sandals
- Flats
- Heels

Health and Safety Needs

- First Aid Kit
- OTC Medicines
- Prescription Medicines
- Sunscreen
- Sunglasses
- Allergy Medications
- EpiPen
- Health Insurance Card
- Eyeglasses

Dr. Melissa Caudle

Electronics

- Flashlight
- Computer
- iPad
- Phone
- Bluetooth Speaker
- Sun Charger
- Charging Block
- Cords
- Selfie Stick
- Headphones
- Portable Fan
- Camera

Decorations

- Door Magnets
- Plagues
- Whiteboard
- Streamers

Miscellaneous

- Book to Read
- Waterproof Case for Phone
- Beach Bag
- Beach Towel Clips
- Magnetic Hooks
- Duct Tape
- Umbrella
- Backpack
- Lanyard for Cruise Card
- Lanyard for Phone
- Beach Bag
- Bug Repellant
- Stain Remover
- Laundry Detergent
- Fiber Absorbent Towel
- Water Bottle
- Ear Plugs
- Eye Mask

ESSENTIALS

- Driver's License
- Money
- Travel Documents
- Credit Cards
- Boarding Pass
- COVID Test Results
- Vaccination Card
- Purse
- Wallet

Cruising Tips & Hacks from a Professional Cruise Addict

CRUISE PLANNING GUIDE

Cruise Line: _____ **Date of Cruise:** _____
Booking #: _____ **Transportation to Port:** _____
Travel Agent: _____ **Phone:** ( ) _____
Celebration: _____
Traveling Companions: _____
_____
_____
_____

Day 1 Destination: _____

    Excursion: _____

    What to wear during the day: _____

    What to wear during the evening: _____

Day 2 Destination: _____

    Excursion: _____

    What to wear: _____

    What to wear during the evening: _____

Day 3 Destination: _____

Excursion: _____

    What to wear: _____

Day 4 Destination: _____

    Excursion: _____

    What to wear: _____

Day 5 Destination: _____

    Excursion: _____

    What to wear: _____

Day 6 Destination: _____

    Excursion: _____

    What to wear: _____

Day 7 Destination: _____

    Excursion: _____

    What to wear: _____

Notes:

_____
_____
_____
_____
_____
_____
_____

Cruising Tips & Hacks from a Professional Cruise Addict

PACKING CHECKLIST

Cruise Line: _____ Date of Cruise: _____
Booking #: _____ Number of Days: _____
Port: _____ Transportation to Port: _____
Destination: _____
Celebration: _____

ESSENTIALS

- Driver's License
- Money
- Travel Documents
- Credit Cards
- Boarding Pass
- COVID Test Results
- Vaccination Card
- Purse
- Wallet

Toiletries

- Toothbrush
- Toothpaste
- Mouthwash
- Shampoo
- Conditioner
- Deodorant
- Razor
- Shaving Cream
- Sunscreen
- Body Lotion
- Aloe Lotion
- Contact Case
- Lip Balm
- Makeup
- Hair Ties
- Bobby Pins
- Makeup Remover
- Styling Gel
- Hairspray

Beach Clothing

- Bathing Suits
- Cover up
- Flip flops
- Water shoes

Dr. Melissa Caudle

Personal Clothing

- Panties
- Bras
- Pajamas
- Socks

Daywear

- 2 Shorts
- 1 Jean
- 2 T-shirts
- 1 Tank Tops

Evening Wear

- 1 Formal Night Attire
- 5 Casual

Outerwear

- Sweater
- Rain Poncho

Shoes

- Tennis Shoes
- Flipflops
- Sandals
- Flats
- Heels

Health and Safety Needs

- First Aid Kit
- OTC Medicines
- Prescription Medicines
- Sunscreen
- Sunglasses
- Allergy Medications
- EpiPen
- Health Insurance Card
- Eyeglasses

Cruising Tips & Hacks from a Professional Cruise Addict

Electronics

- Flashlight
- Computer
- iPad
- Phone
- Bluetooth Speaker
- Sun Charger
- Charging Block
- Cords
- Selfie Stick
- Headphones
- Portable Fan
- Camera

Decorations

- Door Magnets
- Plagues
- Whiteboard
- Streamers

Miscellaneous

- Book to Read
- Waterproof Case for Phone
- Beach Bag
- Beach Towel Clips
- Magnetic Hooks
- Duct Tape
- Umbrella
- Backpack
- Lanyard for Cruise Card
- Lanyard for Phone
- Beach Bag
- Bug Repellant
- Stain Remover
- Laundry Detergent
- Fiber Absorbent Towel
- Water Bottle
- Ear Plugs
- Eye Mask

ESSENTIALS

- Driver's License
- Money
- Travel Documents
- Credit Cards
- Boarding Pass
- COVID Test Results
- Vaccination Card
- Purse
- Wallet

Dr. Melissa Caudle

CRUISE PLANNING GUIDE

Cruise Line: _____   Date of Cruise: _____
Booking #: _____   Transportation to Port: _____
Travel Agent: _____ Phone: (   ) _____
Celebration: _____
Traveling Companions: _____
_____
_____
_____

Day 1 Destination: _____

    Excursion: _____

    What to wear during the day: _____

    What to wear during the evening: _____

Day 2 Destination: _____

    Excursion: _____

    What to wear: _____

    What to wear during the evening: _____

Day 3 Destination: _____

Excursion: _____

    What to wear: _____
Day 4 Destination: _____

Cruising Tips & Hacks from a Professional Cruise Addict

    Excursion: _____

    What to wear: _____

Day 5 Destination: _____

    Excursion: _____

    What to wear: _____

Day 6 Destination: _____

    Excursion: _____

    What to wear: _____

Day 7 Destination: _____

    Excursion: _____

    What to wear: _____

Notes:

_____
_____
_____
_____
_____
_____
_____
_____

Dr. Melissa Caudle

PACKING CHECKLIST

Cruise Line: _____ Date of Cruise: _____
Booking #: _____ Number of Days: _____
Port: _____ Transportation to Port: _____
Destination: _____
Celebration: _____

ESSENTIALS

- Driver's License
- Money
- Travel Documents
- Credit Cards
- Boarding Pass
- COVID Test Results
- Vaccination Card
- Purse
- Wallet

Toiletries

- Toothbrush
- Toothpaste
- Mouthwash
- Shampoo
- Conditioner
- Deodorant
- Razor
- Shaving Cream
- Sunscreen
- Body Lotion
- Aloe Lotion
- Contact Case
- Lip Balm
- Makeup
- Hair Ties
- Bobby Pins
- Makeup Remover
- Styling Gel
- Hairspray

Beach Clothing

- Bathing Suits
- Cover up
- Flip flops
- Water shoes

Cruising Tips & Hacks from a Professional Cruise Addict

Personal Clothing

- Panties
- Bras
- Pajamas
- Socks

Daywear

- 2 Shorts
- 1 Jean
- 2 T-shirts
- 1 Tank Tops

Evening Wear

- 1 Formal Night Attire
- 5 Casual

Outerwear

- Sweater
- Rain Poncho

Shoes

- Tennis Shoes
- Flipflops
- Sandals
- Flats
- Heels

Health and Safety Needs

- First Aid Kit
- OTC Medicines
- Prescription Medicines
- Sunscreen
- Sunglasses
- Allergy Medications
- EpiPen
- Health Insurance Card
- Eyeglasses

Dr. Melissa Caudle

Electronics

- Flashlight
- Computer
- iPad
- Phone
- Bluetooth Speaker
- Sun Charger
- Charging Block
- Cords
- Selfie Stick
- Headphones
- Portable Fan
- Camera

Decorations

- Door Magnets
- Plagues
- Whiteboard
- Streamers

Miscellaneous

- Book to Read
- Waterproof Case for Phone
- Beach Bag
- Beach Towel Clips
- Magnetic Hooks
- Duct Tape
- Umbrella
- Backpack
- Lanyard for Cruise Card
- Lanyard for Phone
- Beach Bag
- Bug Repellant
- Stain Remover
- Laundry Detergent
- Fiber Absorbent Towel
- Water Bottle
- Ear Plugs
- Eye Mask

ESSENTIALS

- Driver's License
- Money
- Travel Documents
- Credit Cards
- Boarding Pass
- COVID Test Results
- Vaccination Card
- Purse
- Wallet

ABOUT THE AUTHOR

"Live a life you love and love your family and you will leave this world happy." **Dr. Melissa Caudle**

Dr. Melissa Caudle, AKA Dr. Mel, is an American award-winning author and screenwriter of more than a hundred books, both fiction and non-fiction, numerous articles in magazines as a freelance writer, and over twenty screenplays. She is also the CEO of Absolute Author Publishing House and has helped hundreds of authors reach their publishing dreams. She is best known for her novels *The Keystroke Killer: Transcendence, A.D.A.M. The Beginning of Life, Never Stop Running,* and *Secret Romances: The Forbidden Thirst for Love.* She also authors children's educational books and fiction books including *The Creek Dweller in the Bayou* which is currently in production as an animated film

As an artist, Dr. Mel illustrates adult coloring books in her series *Abstract Faces* which include several her favorite art creations and many other styles including mandalas, animals, and flowers. She describes her style of art as a mixture between Picasso and Salvador Dali. She uses professional markers, acrylic paints, and watercolors. Take a look for yourself below.

Dr. Mel's hobbies include drawing, composing music, and collecting marbles, both antique and contemporary. She lives in New Orleans, LA with her husband and two cats. She is the mother of three daughters and has seven grandsons and one granddaughter. When she is not writing or drawing, she loves to take cruises, go to the New Orleans Saints games, ballroom dance, swim, camping, and spend time with her family. Her goal is to keep living life to the fullest and cherish every moment.

For more information, check out Dr. Mel's website at www.drmelcaudle.com and subscribe to her blog at www.drmelcaudle.blogspot.com which has over 13 million in readership. Also, follow her on her social media sites.

https://twitter.com/#!/DrMelcaudle

https://www.facebook.com/DrMelCaudle

https://www.facebook.com/The Keystroke Killer Fan Site

linkedin.com/in/dr-mel-caudle-650a4036

ADULT COLORING BOOKS

One of my hobbies, other than writing, is drawing abstract faces in a Picasso kind of way. I put together my favorites in a series of Adult Coloring Books. You can buy them on Amazon, Barnes and Noble, and on my website: www.drmelcaudle.com, and other online retailers.

Novels by Dr. Melissa Caudle for Your Cruise Reading

The Keystroke Killer: Transcendence

New Orleans – 2058 - MATTHEW RAYMOND, a private investigator, locked into a maze of deceit and deception, uncovers the truth of Project Transcendence.

For Matthew Raymond, his job as a private investigator is personal. Extremely personal. After the disturbing 2053 murder of his sister Livia, Matthew left in a rage, searches for her killer and answers to the mysterious questions that lurked around her death. Now, years later, Matthew realizes his problems just went from bad to worse as he discovers himself immersed in a city where the wealthy and corrupt politicians rule. With his sister's murder still his focus, he finds himself in a cunning game of cat-and-mouse when he stumbles across The Keystroke Killer and uncovers a secret device capable of sending people to the fourth dimension without a trace. Project Transcendence becomes Matthew's new fixation. Searching the Deep South for answers, he uncovers family secrets, lies, corruption and a world on the brink of destruction. Can Matthew survive and save the world from the threat? Will he untangle the mystery of Livia's death? Find out in this compelling story, *The Keystroke Killer*.

BUY NOW ON AMAZON BY SCANNING QR CODE

A.D.A.M.

By Dr. Melissa Caudle

A scientist. An alien lifeform. A secret base.

Consequences for mankind.

Meet Dr. Sandra Eve Bradford, an astrobiological researcher in charge of the A.D.A.M. Extraction Team who discovers a microbe which thrives off arsenic on the bottom of Mono Lake in California. General Anbar, in charge of the U.S. National Defense, orders his team to confiscate the samples and her research. Dr. Bradford enlists her fellow researchers, Dr. Gregory Peterson, and her undergraduate assistant, Jessica Parker, to retrieve a new sample which set off a series of events and consequences.

In a government research facility, the microbe transforms into something alien. Once it becomes apparent to General Anbar the life form presents a national security risk, he orders his men to kidnap Dr. Bradford and holds her captive in an underground facility to continue her research.

The lifeform over a seven-day stretch, morphs into a human-like lifeform aging every moment toward death. His journey makes him question - What is life? What is love? What is hate? And, is there a God? This a story of possibilities and raises the questions - Are we alone in the universe? What else could be out there?

BUY NOW ON AMAZON BY SCANNING QR CODE

Dr. Melissa Caudle

Never Stop Running

What happens when the unthinkable occurs? What would you do if your loved one a suddenly woke up and didn't know who you were or for that matter who your family was either? For David and Jackie Hennessey, they had the perfect white picket fence life, marriage, family, and careers until the unthinkable happened - an accident that left Jackie with no memory. The couple struggles to find the balance between what they once shared and their new life. After David discovers Dr. Grayson, a well-known regression hypnotherapist, he convinces Jackie to seek his services to retrieve her repressed memories. During her sessions, her memories surface only to uncover her past lives which crisscross centuries in her mental time travel. Faced with a moral dilemma of believing the dreams were once a reality and twisting her religious convictions on reincarnation, Jackie questions her sanity and fears for her life after seeing her deaths in her previous lives. She believes she could never stop running as her marriage degrades and falls apart. Based on real events of hypnotic regression sessions of one brave woman, this is a tale of destiny and soulmates not to be missed. The most intriguing book you'll read all year. You don't have to believe in reincarnation to enjoy this tale, but it will get you to thinking about the possibility.

BUY NOW ON AMAZON BY SCANNING QR CODE

RECOMMENDED READING

Dear Readers:

Although I did not write this book, I had the pleasure of editing and publishing this book with my company, Absolute Author Publishing House. I consider this a must-read book and will be perfect for your cruse time reading! Order your copy today!

SCAN ME

Printed in Great Britain
by Amazon